The Glass Window

◆

The Glass Window

◆

Compiled by Mario Morales
Cover design & Graphics
by Michelle M. Morales

Authors Choice Press
San Jose New York Lincoln Shanghai

The Glass Window

Authors Choice Press
an imprint of iUniverse.com, Inc.

For information address:
iUniverse.com, Inc.
5220 S 16th, Ste. 200
Lincoln, NE 68512
www.iuniverse.com

Some of the names have been changed out of respect for the individuals mentioned and who wish to remain anonymous. My thanks to them for the reasons that I built mistrust and burned many bridges. Perhaps we can rebuild these bridges as I rebuild my life. They know not that I am still a friend.

ISBN: 0-595-19726-4

Printed in the United States of America

Dedication

◆

To my wife Joanie, what a wonderful person, she always gave me all the rope I needed. Thank you for being there for me during the hard times, standing by me and having faith in me to do the right thing. She is a special type of woman, who doesn't come around every day. You're understanding and patience helped me to heal on my own.

To my parents: bittersweet is life at times, we know we try our best. Bitter is the life we sometimes live, sweet is to have existed at all.

Contents

◆

Foreword

◆

I really admire the author and his success when his life could have gone the wrong way. My hope would be that boys in Junior High could read this book and see that a better life can become reality.

Carolyn Klemme
Social Services Agency
Training and Career Development

The Glass Window by Mario Morales

- Mr. Morales manuscript is a testimony to the resilience of his human spirit in growing up in inner city area of Orange County, California
- Mario Morales book provides insights into the challenges faced by youth growing up in inner city areas of this society—in this case, Santa Ana, California
- Truly an inspirational account!

Comments by: **Mikel Hogan-Garcia, Ph.D.**

The Glass Window is Great! It makes you sad, it makes you angry, and it makes you think & appreciate the life you have! Once I started reading it, I couldn't put it down

Diana Munoz
County of Orange
Social Services Agency

This is a truly inspirational book for anyone who has or is going down the dark side and thinks this is the way, the only way. There are other ways out, and this book proves it.

Fabiola Lopez
Social Services Agency

The Glass Window
A compelling autobiography of a courageous child, going through life is carrying the pain and anger after being abused. Then these feelings manifest into self-destruction. A great educational tool for pre-teen children.

Rosa Rubalcava
Social Services Agency

A compelling story of this man's struggles in life. It was very intense and will leave the reader with a feeling of hope that maybe others will follow the right path in life.

Maricela Avalos
Social Services Agency

The Glass Window
Wow! What a truly inspirational story. I only hope that this book can be shared so that it can touch others as it touched me. If you didn't

believe in the power of LOVE and healing of faith, you will after reading this touching story.

Renee Ruiz
Social Services Agency

The Glass Window

In my opinion, **The Glass Window** *should be standard reference work for anyone dealing with the problems of young people. It makes one realize that the so-called, "bad kids" did not just happen—rather they are often victims of circumstances beyond their control. A little understanding and counseling can go a long way in turning a life around.*

Maya B. Fischer, BA

Having an opportunity to read this book was an eye opening experience. It exposed me to a lot of things that go on in your very own neighborhood. The author shows a great amount of courage and resiliency by sharing his life story with us.

Odon Sanchez
Social Services Agency

The Glass Window

This true history offers hope for recovery, and help for the young people so they can continue into adulthood with a great sense of self and well being. This book helps me to increase my knowledge in the class I am taking in "Human Services" especially counseling the families of addicted persons. I hope that others will read this book so that it can touch others lives as it did to me.

Olga Rifaat
Social Services Agency

"Grippingly intense" "mind boggling" A raw, compelling first hand account of a person's downward spiral—from an innocent child to an accused killer. This is an intense look at the life of a person whose choices, almost immediately, following a particular, severe trauma, became pointedly self-destructive. It also allows a realistic glimpse into the day to day life of an addict chronicled in a matter-of-fact, yet unforgettable story.

Mario—I wish you well.   **Cindy Morales**

This is one serious autobiography of a man's life. To go through everything he did and survive, proves and says it all. Never Give Up! Writing this book the way everything happened straight out was the way to do it. Peace Mario!

Diane Morones
Social Services Agency

Having the misfortune of living a part of my life that identifies and relates to "The Glass Window", it's contents are eerily accurate and it's story is so compelling that I found myself anxious to get to the next page. And knowing Mr. Morales personally for most of my life gave me a quick lesson in judging character cause there are aspects and dimensions to an old friend that I had no knowledge. All in all, "The Glass

Window" is a story that needed to be told and should be an inspiration to the youth of today. A lesson in overcoming adversity.

Donald Aguilar

I can relate and understand the story, because I went through the same things with my sons. If more stories like this would come out in other people's lives, it would help kids to realize what drugs do to them before they get into the wrong pattern of life.

Della Aguilar
Mother of seven children.

Mr. Morales paints a picture with his words. You are compelled to listen and feel from page one. His book gives you rich history and a gamut of emotions. You feel his pain and anguish as well as his revelations of his soul.

This book is a guide for those stuck in the mire of institutionalization and drug abuse, they can read this and free their minds.

Corliss Graham
Social Services

The Glass Window
Encouraging true testimony from an individual that I admire and respect, I feel fortunate to work with Mario. Holding on to hope and searching for answers. I can hardly wait until his book is published, as I would like to share this book with my relatives and friends.

Esperanza Saunas
Social Services Agency

A traumatic testimony given to be told at such a tender age to suppress instead of exposing this secret and not given a choice to voice his feelings. Mario—your courage and discipline is to be admired.

Lola DeLaRiva

An inspirational story of a courageous man who had the strength to turn his life around. "The Glass Window", not only serves as a light of hope for those venturing down the same dark tunnel as the author did, but also as a wake-up call for those who haven't seen this 'tunnel' & forget to appreciate how fortunate they are for that.

Karishma Tejwani
High School Student

A sensitive, encompassing and accountable testimony that recognizes and honors our relationship and connection with all things. A gift to be passed along and shared so that any of us who are touched by these revelations, may somehow benefit by our common humanness, and not feel alone in doing so. Thank you Mario for sharing your gift, that God-Self, the higher consciousness that prevails within the core of us all. Thank you for remembering and reminding us of who we are.

For All My Relations Brother
Cheryl Parke
SSA/Child Abuse Registry

In "The Glass Window", Mario Morales has written a truth that some can only imagine and those who can relate will be moved beyond words. I applaud his triumph over such great adversity and believe that through his courage many will be inspired.

Cathy Sena
Department of Social Services

Wow!…I cried for Mr. Morales, or for myself, I am really not sure which. I thank him for sharing his life and letting some light through the window, not only for himself but also for all of us who have read, or will read, this heart wrenching but wonderful story…Aun aye esperanza.

Nicolas Sena
Procurement Agent
Boeing Aircraft Co.

"The Glass Window" was riveting, frightening at times, I was cheering for Mario to over come his addiction and behavior patterns. I couldn't put the book down. Thumbs up! He conquered the beast and won!

Judie Manuel
Social Services

Mario, you are definitely an inspiration to our society. I admire your courage to share such a valuable piece of your history's life living. I pictured all your surroundings, felt your pain, and your strength to move into a better life. Being born in Orange County and raised in Santa Ana myself, your history has made me reminisce Santa Ana's history as well. Congratulations and I hope to see this story in a movie series some day.

Best wishes and good luck,

Alicia Ramirez
Social Services.

"The Glass Window" was an inspirational story of one man's trial and tribulation, who despite many obstacles succeed in what can be said, a truly amazing journey.

Victor Salas
County of Orange

I started to read Mr. Morales' book and found my eyes glued to the pages. It captured my attention and I really felt his story was moving. At some parts, I teared up at the intense emotion in his words. It takes strength to tell a tale of hardships and pain, and I commend Mr. Morales for wanting others to know about him. I hope everything turns out success-ful for him and his book!

Sarah Carmona
Senior, Irvine High School

What an inspirational book, a true testimonial. Mario, the changes that occurred in your life because of the love and grace of God, doors were opened to you. I know this book will be an inspiration to many. God Bless You.

Mary Jo O'Rourke

I enjoyed reading about Santa Ana, the way it was in the old days. The garage parties. I went to Franklin Street in 1958. The movie shows down town, and Pringles.

All I can say is congratulations; I'm proud of you and hope your book will help some kids that are on the path of self-destruction.

Thanks,
Wilhelmina Gordon

The Glass Window expressed heart-warming situations that related to my family and me. I feel whoever reads this book will get a great inspiration to keep going in life and not give up.

Ann Williams

Be prepared, this book will stir your emotions! The author provides an honest and in-depth view of the impact of childhood trauma on the adult survivor…A valuable resource for both clinician and survivor.

Lynn Meineke
Economic and Community Partnerships

Preface

—————— ◆ ——————

Born and raised in Southern California I grew up in a world of heavy confusion in a nation in the midst of Cultural Revolution. Being born in the 50's, I am considered one of the children of the Atomic Age. I grew up as a person, not recognizing any ethnic barriers. If I were to name ethnic backgrounds, I would be a Native American of Mexican and Irish decent.

I didn't write this book for any ethnic considerations. It is for the children. The children we don't discuss in public or in the open. There are many children out there using drugs or on the verge of suicide or have already tried. It's too late for those who have succeeded, but not for their families. This book is for those survivors with an open ear. I must reach these children no matter how far back in life they go or how old they are. This is for them.

Acknowledgements

$\blacklozenge$

To all the people in Social Services who became friends, for their encouraging thoughts and ideas and not realizing how proud I am to work with such a wonderful group of individuals until this story is told.

To my wife Joanie, whose love and support endeavored to persevere.

To my daughter Addy, who without her radiance, I would not be writing this book.

To my son Xavier, for teaching me how to be a man, friend and father and keeping me entertained.

To my sister Christine, living in an institution most of her life has survived and now living in peace and contentment, God bless her.

To my brothers Michael and Monnie who have always been my big brothers although I am taller than they are.

To my brother-in-law Gilbert and sister Cathy for trying so hard to help me when I wasn't ready.

To Ben & Chris Libay, for being such good friends, mentors and peers and a source of encouragement.

To my little brother Mark who will always be my little brother.

To my brother-in-law Alex and Sister Monica for their trust and faith and helping when most needed.

To all, whose life may have been affected by my actions, I apologize, especially to my brothers and sisters.

The Mirror Darkly
(Revelations)
◆

1985, Orange County California, after years of drug abuse, Jails, Hospitals, Institutions, and yes, even death, I found myself, once again, in the Orange County Jail, arrested for the California Penal Code 187, murder. It was the darkest period of my life and reality was delivering a crushing blow on me, slowly chewing at my soul, with the torment of insanity on the verge of busting out of my innermost being. All my past was catching up with me and together, alone, again in a house full of prisoners. My gut wanted to spill over and vomit and common sense told me to speak to no one. They didn't trust me and I didn't trust them. The difficulty was the mistrust of inmates wanting to know if I was planted to gather information before it was known that I was a regular. Eventually someone would vouch for you who would know you from the streets or previously did time together somewhere. With all this, I didn't care; I was starting to get sick without a fix after about 18 hours of county process. I went through the booking process, shaking me down for contraband, one phone call, filing out forms, understanding my rights, showering, getting sprayed for lice and getting a new set of jail house issue clothing, and I was tired. The trustee inmates knew I was not a fish, and at least I got a new jumpsuit, shorts, tee shirt, socks and tennis shoes. After the countless questions by the Sheriffs

Department and the uncertainty of my future, I finally reached my cell. An overcrowded eight-man cell with up to fourteen men at times. The only room was underneath the television in the day room where I dropped my bedroll and lay there for awhile I told myself to forget everything from here on out cause it's going to be a different life. I fell asleep for a few hours, which seemed like minutes and was awakened later by inmates making coffee. Using the outlet right above my head, with two razor blades for a *stinger*, each blade connected to wires to make a heating element and an inmate excusing himself for spilling a few drops of water on me. It makes you wonder, how they get all that stuff in here, but inmates are very resourceful. They even had a telephone in the cell. A telephone of which I'm sure took many writs and countless hours of resource material to obtain. There was a table for eight, a shower, toilet/sink combination, stainless steel mirror, telephone and television in the day room, which was connected by an inner door to the eight-man bunk area. If you wanted to take your chances, you could just kick someone out of the bunk area and take his spot, but usually it's much wiser to wait your turn.

I was asked, "what you busted for *ESE*?" still half-asleep and keeping one eye open, I told him, "a *muerte.*" It got quiet for a second, then they said, "you want some coffee eh!" Later, I would show them my booking slip when one of the inmates asked, "can I see your booking slip *eh*? I never seen one with a *muerte* on it!" When I showed it to him, I hoped it would sink in and they would know I wasn't a jail house *snitch*. He said, "*Chingao! Homes!* You in for some big time *eh*!" I knew that by the time we went to the *chowhall*, I would recognize someone I knew or they would recognize me either in the vestibule or the *chowhall* and I would get confirmation that I was OK. Jail is where you see all the people you haven't seen in years. You see people you went to the same school with. You know who they are, but not by name. They disappear and years later, you see why. They're in jail for one offense or another. This place of concrete and steel seems like a gathering place for lost souls of times gone by, but not without a sense of misplaced irony. It took about eight days before I could stop vomiting and eat and the sweats were receding. There was one other inmate in my cell that was in for murder. He got released about three months later and I believe it was for lack of evidence. That day was a big hurrah for our cell as we all had a sense of getting over on the system and hope entered our lives if even for a brief moment.

By that time, I was receiving regular visits from my wife Joanie and daughter Addy. The Deputy announced my name over the loudspeaker for a visit. It makes you feel good to get a visit, but this visit wasn't going to be what I expected. My daughter was about nineteen months old at the time and very vocal. We were in the visiting section, with rows of booths, each with one half-inch glass in an archway about four feet tall with a phone attached to the side of it. All around were posted signs saying, "Warning! Your phone calls may be monitored at any time". I remember I was an emotional mess, blaming myself on one hand and on the other regretting what I was doing to my family and how I was going to deal with the present situation. I told my wife that I didn't think I was going to get out-ever. On the other hand, maybe I'd be away for a very long time- or dead. I also told her that I didn't want my daughter growing up without a role model or a father figure to look up too. "A fine time to think about that one" I told myself. My wife Joanie started to cry at the thought and I told her, it would probably be best to get a divorce and for her to marry someone else who could take care of my daughter, Addy. God! The pain I felt, when I said that, failing myself being a father, husband and friend. I felt a total loss and wanted to separate myself from feeling anything. I was good at hiding feelings. I didn't know what was right or wrong anymore. I just felt trapped and wished this bad dream would go away and all the time knowing it was as real as the jumpsuit I was in. Joanie insisted that she would stay by me and insisted we not take that path. My daughter Addy could feel her mother's pain and see her demeanor change. She also recognized the pain in my eyes, and with her little body, stood on the shelf of the glass window, pounding it, with her tiny fist, and yelling, "Ta-Ta open up! Ta-Ta open up!" She was so young, she couldn't say daddy or Poppa, and it came out Ta-Ta. I let out a long drawn out sigh and somehow, those words hit deep into the back of my brain and heavy into my very soul. I was a fool and upset at myself and it was getting worse. Now I had another feeling I had to bury in a place that was out of room. How could anyone know what it's like to let yourself go so far as to end up in a place like this? All because I couldn't control my drug use. Because I lived in a world where I was the enemy, an addict, scum of the earth. All I had to put up with just to get the next fix. All the time running from nowhere and going no place-and I worked hard at it. Nowhere was a deep, dark secret of a frightened child in a man's body trying to burst out and crack my brain. Burning every bridge, I built on friendship and loyalty—trusting no one. That's what got me here and I was mad as hell. I knew I had no one to blame but myself and I had no excuse but for the establishment keeping me working good jobs with little pay and an average of sixty hours per week Getting burned out taking uppers to go to work, and downers to come home.

One of the bridges I burned was with God. "Don't go there", the back of my mind kept saying. As in many times before, I turned to him when I was in need, just to turn around and go back to the drug scene. I no longer wanted to ask for help knowing I would do it again, it pained me to do so. I was tired of asking as I felt him trying to creep up on me. I put God out of my mind and my heart. With all these thoughts, I just wanted to lay down and go to sleep.

By this time, I was more familiar with my *cellies*, and my body was beginning to heal after *detoxing* cold turkey and I could be more rational in my thinking. I found out that the guy I was in there for was a *snitch*. Some people of his own kind wanted him badly. He had a knife shoved up his nose in the San Quentin yard. I had always wondered how he got that scar and I found out people wanted him dead. Not knowing, I was hailed as some sort of hero. Sick, ain't it?

"Reveille! Reveille! Reveille! All inmates up for the standing count! Full jail issue!" shouted the loudspeaker. I hated getting up at 4:00 a.m. for standing count. Not because it was a standing count, but we had to get ready for breakfast release. It was a ritual, washing faces, brushing teeth; getting dressed and wait…wait for the release. It was the time for preparing all inmates for breakfast and those that are due in court that day or transferred to other courts in various cities. A long process of counts, *dressing out* or getting chained up for transfer. We moved slowly when the deputy called on our module for breakfast and opened the electric steel doors to be released into the vestibule. The vestibule, where the tension is so thick, you can cut it with a knife. In this part of the county jail, which is called "Mod-C", all inmates have previously been to state prison or are going to be again. Our cells are segregated; it's the way it is. I never agreed with this issue. Although the state segregates, the county does also, but only in the cells and not in the chow hall. This can create some very disturbing situations. Segregation does have its advantages, like safety in numbers. You never know when something is going to kick off, but you can feel it and your senses have to be on alert. The vestibule is where things happened and usually where somebody gets whacked. You don't know what transpired the night before, or who was new, or who had a grudge or death wish that had to be settled before the night was through. I always got this sickening feeling in my gut. Fear pulsing through my body. Suddenly aware I had a heartbeat, thumping to get out. "Why do I have to go through all this bull just to go eat breakfast?" I told myself. "Set it aside and go for it, we got to eat sometime" I thought.

Everyday was a game. What group was going to go first, the whites, the blacks, or the browns? This one morning the blacks went first and the whites and browns were mixed. Like I said, the inmates preferred segregation, but the county deputies liked to mix tables racially and the seating is four to a table. The deputy in charge would seat you row by row just after you pick-up your meal from under the stainless steal wall, where the food handlers were. Crazy, this white guy from Long Beach, who was in for robberies and later escaped, was in front of me and he got seated at a table with three black guys. I was seated on the next table at the following row at the other end of the chow hall. Crazy didn't like the idea too well and began to complain. I started eating my meal in a hurry 'cause I could see what was going to happen next. The deputy in charge told Crazy that if he didn't like it, he could pick-up his tray and go back to his cell without eating. He did, and I saw the deputy heading my way. I didn't know that what was about to transpire next would change my life forever. "Pick it up and move down", the deputy said to me in a commanding tone of voice as he pointed to the now empty seat where Crazy was. I said, "No! I'm eating", and I could not believe I said that, it just came out. The deputy didn't expect that answer, and well, that did it. Have you ever been in a mess hall and heard all the noises and the hum of talking and clatter of trays with commotion? Well, when I said that, it got so quiet in there, that the inmates at the other end of the chow hall, who didn't know what was going on, felt the change in the air. They were looking to see what happened. The deputy was immediately on the hand radio calling for back up. My cellies, who were at my table, were giving me the sign to set it off and start a riot. Having more sense than that and being drug free for a few months, I had my wits about me. I gave my cellie a mean glance, and said, "it's my call!" The other deputies began to arrive at my table and we were surrounded. The deputy received a call on the radio then asked for my booking slip and I gave it to him. I continued to eat heartily, although now I didn't feel like it. He radioed the *bubble* and got instructions to physically remove my tray. When the deputy started to reach for my tray, I couldn't believe he was going to do it. I said in a very convincing and menacing voice, "Don't! Even! Touch my tray!" He backed off and I was relieved for the moment. The Deputy proceeded radioing and receiving instructions from some unknown force or source of information. He then told me that the sergeant wanted to speak with me in the *bubble.* I told the deputy, "tell the sergeant, that as soon as I'm done with my meal, I'll go talk to him". The Deputy radioed back to the *bubble* and I ate slower now, trying to figure out my next move or how I was going to act. I didn't want to get all crazy, but this is like trying to organize chaos. Many people try to organize chaos everyday, but this could cost you your life. It was like a chess game, and in this chess game, I knew that if I won, I would lose. I ate even more slowly now but minutes turned to seconds. I told my *cellies*, "I'll ride it out, it's my call". I could see the fear and hate in the eyes of the deputies as they looked around nervously, ready for violence. I wanted them to sweat, to feel what it's like to be scared and in short, learn a lesson. When I was ready, I told the deputy I was done and they were keeping a close eye on me. Four deputies escorted me to see the sergeant in the *bubble.* Along with the relief, I also felt a sense of power as I got signs of approval from the inmates as I was being led out of the *chowhall.* Just like in the movie, "Cool Hand Luke", it was like a solidarity thing to get over on the system and authority. The sad part is that it was sick attention and although I was drug free, I was still sick.

I waited outside at the *bubble. I* knew the sergeant was giving me time to cool off, but I was cool and ready. In my mind I thought the deputies were going to take me in the elevator and beat on me for awhile, later you'll know why, but setting that aside I waited. He opened the door and called me in and asked me if I was who the booking slip said I was, and I said, "yes, that's me". He said, "what are you trying to do?" "No!" I said, "what are your deputies trying to do? Your deputies are the ones who screwed up! Did you even see? What would you have me do? When the inmate who didn't want to eat went back to his cell and I saw the deputy come towards me, *I knew what time it was.* What if I had gotten up and moved, would you have to move the person next to me and then the person next to that person and so on down the line. He would've had to move the whole *chowhall* by the time he realized his mistake". The sergeant remained quiet, hand on chin, thinking for a few moments. I didn't want him to see that I was scared and in another way, I didn't care. He broke the silence, "you know your right", he said. "Damn right I'm right, I said. "But you know, I still have to discipline you for refusing a directive", he said. In my mind, I said, "it's always the little guy that gets it". "Yea! Sure! I know", I said. I could see the wheels working in the sergeant's head, not knowing for sure how to handle this situation. He looked to me more friendly than angry, and I'm sure he wasn't going to like writing the incident report. I always wondered how he did write up that report, whether his deputies were disciplined or not. The inmates were the ones suffering, for their indiscriminate ways. I waited outside for the lieutenant to come and confer with the sergeant. When it was over, I was called in and told, "10 days in the hole, then you'll be returned back to the main population". I smiled and thought to myself, "I can do that standing on my head". There I go again, head up, acting cool and strolling like a hard ass. Deep inside I was kicking myself and saying to myself, "here's another fine mess you got yourself into!"

After a short while, I was met by a Deputy who took me to a clothing room where I traded my official mustered colored jumpsuit for a, "your in the hole", burgundy color jumpsuit. The hole was downstairs, which was split-leveled in the center of the building. On the outer side were solid steel doors with a tray slot about knee level. An inner door was barred, so it took two sets of doors to get to the inner cell. The whole section echoed with banging steel against steel and jingling sounds of keys or doors being locked or unlocked. The cells are about six by nine feet and three more feet to the outer door. When I was led in, the deputy said, "you get a bedroll for the night, but have to give it back in the morning". I always thought they didn't have bedrolls at all, so I was fine with that. I remember the sound of them closing the door with a loud bang, echoing away at the walls until all went silent. After a moment of silence, I said, "Finally! I get some time to myself!" It was a relief to get away from the main population and I did need the time to think. I looked around the cell, I had a toilet/sink combination where I could wash or drink water. There was a roll of toilet paper and a small sliver of soap. "That'll come in handy", I thought. I wasn't in there but a minute, when there was loud banging that vibrated through the whole block and an inmate was yelling at the top of his lungs. It really sounded like he was mad, mad at the world and purging his soul of hatred and anguish. I was soon to find out for myself. The inmate who was yelling was in a different type of cell and could get right up to the solid door with a tray slot for receiving meals. My cell had an inner cell and I couldn't reach the door or see out very well. The steel door had a small window, not big enough to get your body through, and it had cross bars in it, which means you couldn't get your arm through it, even if it were somehow busted open. It got quiet again, and as I sat on the metal bed. All I could hear was the whirring sound of the exhaust fan above my head. It seemed as if I could almost see the air being stirred round and round, with a rustling motion going right through my head. I tried to block it out with thoughts, but at the moment, my thoughts only brought despair and I tried to block that out too.

After the second day and at the evening mealtime, I could hear the clatter and jingling of keys going from cell to cell delivering the meal. When my cell door was opened, an inmate trustee brought the meal and passed it through the slot in the bars. In passing the plate, he said, "*hora-le homes, aye te va!*" and I took the plate. "Roast beef tonight!" I said loudly. Mashed potatoes and some weird form of vegetables. I was hungry and the beef looked like a healthy serving. As I began to dig in, I looked under the beef covered in gravy. "What the F__k Is that!" I said out loud. It was a pack of smokes. Wow, I was dying for a smoke and I got this big smile on my face, and then realized, I didn't have any matches. "Ahhh! F__k!" I grumbled loudly and began to laugh. Laugh loudly, like I just heard the funniest joke in the world almost with a touch of insanity to it. Here I was in jail, in the jail of the jail, for a murder *beef* and I was laughing over a pack of cigarettes.

Later that evening after our plates were picked up and bedrolls issued for the night, I could hear the inmate that was yelling a few days before. This time, he was singing a Rolling Stones song. A lousy singer too, but with a familiar sound. Then I recognized who it was. "Jimbo! That you?" I yelled.

"Who's that!" he yelled back.

"Your daddy punk!" I retorted.

"Mario! That you?"

"Yea! It's me".

Jimmy Martinez is my second cousin from my mother's side of the family. His father and my grandfather are brothers. Ever since I knew Jimmy, he was always in some kind of trouble. Like me, it was behind drugs or drug related. He came from a family of twelve, lived in the Delhi Barrio in Santa Ana, raised mostly by his mother. For kids growing up there, you had to have a rough n' tumble attitude. It's a social style one must develop which is abrasive, dominant, and controlling.

"Hang in there *primo!*" he yelled. "I heard you got popped for a *muerte*".

"Yea", I said, "got a light?"

"You got *frajos?* "

"Yea",

"I'll send you a line, we're going fishing!" he yelled.

I never had to make a line before. I heard about it and never was in the position to have to make do with what you got. Jimmy knew what to do and after a little coaxing I got a thread from my tee shirt and slowly started to unravel a loose thread at the bottom. I didn't do very well, but after a time I found that my sock seemed to be more cooperative and I got about eight to nine feet of thread out of it. That's all I needed, Jimmy would do the rest. He had his line tied to his pocket comb and under the door flung the comb towards my door. It took a few tries and got his line close enough for me to throw my line under the door and cross his line. Slowly, very slowly I pulled my line until the comb started to cross his and he intern pulled his until our combs created a lock. I pulled his line towards mine and got it under the door. I tied the cigarettes to his line, flat enough to get under the door and told him to pull slowly. He did and we repeated the same process to send the matches. He gave me one half of the striker and some matches. In order to conserve the paper matches, we split them in half to get double the amount. I had to laugh cause we were just like little kids again getting away with something we weren't supposed to do. Only we were in adult bodies now…

I was about the same age as Jimmy and his brother Richard while my mother worked at the Norris Market in Delhi Barrio in the early Sixties. We spent a lot of time together. When we were in high school, both Jimmy and Richard could have been fantastic football players if the drug scene had not gotten in the way. Richard could have also become a prominent bass guitarist and when we were out of school, we played in the garage. While writing this book, Richard passed away. I played the drums and we had another cousin, Danny Barriga, who played lead guitar. This was a time when Jeff Beck, Eric Clapton, Jimmy Hendrix, and the Rolling Stones were hot and the whole blues music scene was turning into a different pop culture. Again, it was powered by drugs and we acted like there's too much blood in our drug system with no fear of dying. All of it was fun. Just look at me now.

Meanwhile, back in the cell was kick back, having a smoke and us trying to keep the demons at bay. I gave Jimmy enough to share with the guy next to him. While they were fishing, I would just lay back and listen to the sounds or reminisce about anything that crossed my mind. It was like doing mental push-ups and I had to keep my mind occupied. I was sitting on my bunk staring at the walls. On the wall across from me, was some writing that was misspelled. It said, "Our Fader in Arth of Heven." I thought about the person who wrote that passage and came to the conclusion that most of the people in here cannot read or write and were hungry for some spiritual salvation or comfort. I thought, "one day I can help them somehow, someway"….

"What am I doing here?" I shouted out loud.

       ✳   ✳   ✳

After sleeping a couple of days, I really didn't feel like sleeping anymore and my waking hours got longer and longer. My thoughts began to clutter and I was getting moody and my disposition turned angry as a flood of thoughts from the past started to enter the picture. I was getting to a point where it became difficult to block them out. Then I caught myself trying to sing. I could never remember most songs unless they were written right there in front of me. All I could remember was some childhood songs from church. I knew "Amazing Grace", but not all of it, so I sang what I knew and made up the rest. I remembered, when I was back in the cellblock with the main population, waiting for unlock for breakfast, when most were sleeping, I was singing the Beatles song "Listen". I got through the whole song where the whole tier could hear it and nobody said a thing. I don't know if it was because they liked the song, thought I was crazy, or were afraid I would go off on them if they did yell out, "Shut up!"

In the next few days it was getting a bit more intense as I began to change, going from one extreme emotion to the other, like positive and negative jolts piercing my very soul. At about the seventh day I was getting tired of this pace where hours and minutes slowed down to a crawl and I was paying the price, no wonder they call it "big time". Time is so precious and so very real that we tend to forget how much until you reach a place like this and find out that either you manage time or time manages you. I felt as if my freedom was taken away like having a disability and the world was suddenly different and hostile from a different point of view.

I could hear banging of metal doors and the keys coming closer to my cell and a deputy opened it up and told me to get dressed for a visit. I thought it was my wife at first, but then remembered, no visits allowed while in the hole. It must be business and it was, I was going to the Attorney Bonds area where inmates confer with lawyers and their foot men investigators. The deputy told me to place my hands through the bars and handcuffed me. Next were the leg chains placed around my ankles and a chain around my waist that was connected to the hand-cuffs with a padlock. Fully secured, they opened the door to my cell and I was led out. Another inmate went with us. He went by the name of Pirate and after he was secured, we went downstairs by way of escalator or elevator and a few controlled lock-up areas where the deputy had to ask for entrance. My lawyer sent his investigator to ask more questions. In essence, the visit was about whether or not I would take a test where I would be hypnotized to help remember the parts where I went into a rage. I told him "sure, anytime", and he said arrangements might be made if necessary. The visit took all of five minutes and it took at least forty-five minutes to get there. Actually, the time out of the cell was a break. When done and another forty-five minutes waiting I was searched again for contraband. On the way back to my cell, I was side tracked and taken back to the sergeant's office. They told me that I just got four more days in the hole. When I was downstairs, they *shook down* my cell and found the cigarettes I had left hiding under the metal bed frame. I cursed myself for being so stupid, but with all the shakedowns, it was also a risk to carry them with me.

Back in the cell, I found myself drifting off. Fantasizing to some distant magic place. Wishing I could dream again. The flying dreams I used to get, taking me places I've never been before. The Buddhists would say that the body is connected to the spirit or soul by three-fold silver cord of life. When you dream it stretches with you in that dream, wherever you want to go. If by chance you encounter a malicious spirit and it happens to scare you, then your spirit returns to your body immediately and you wake up thinking you had a bad dream. The fact is that we don't know that the malicious spirit can't hurt you in the Spirit State unless you let it. If you stand your ground, it will go away and seek some other soul to create havoc and poke fun with devious deeds. They say it is a level of spirituality one must achieve and there are many levels. One of the levels is when a person dies, his soul passes by a man and a woman in the act of making love. If your spirit perceives this as just an act of love then you go on to the next level. If your spirit perceives it as a sexual encounter and it excites you, then your spirit will be drawn into the encounter. The child they conceive will be you, only to be born again and live your life all over again and die again until you can attain the next level.

Although I could never control my direction when flying in the dream very well, I could see clearly and in color at times. Sometimes I would be flying and many times, I've flown towards these towering high-tension wires, like you would see in the countryside or desert. Try as much as I could, I couldn't turn very well when I'd see them coming. In fact, I couldn't go up or down very well either. I'd crash right into the high voltage and I would wake, sometimes saying, "damn, I did it again". Yet, I found myself wishing I were there. Maybe because I no longer had the will to live, a fear of living or even to care what would happen to me? I started to wonder why. Why didn't I care any more? What happened? At first I thought it was easier to just say, "I don't give a f__k about nothin!" I knew that was a lie. It was a mechanism for self-preservation and a character amour to protect my real feelings. Then the thought came, but it was more like a vision of a thought, and I heard, "because you took one of God's children".

"It couldn't be God, because God wouldn't say, you took one of Gods children", I thought. I tried to shut it out and yelled out loud, "No! I know what you're trying to do!" Suddenly, I was awake. My heart was pounding and all the time knowing that I was going to have to open up the subject again. I found myself pacing back and forth in the cell relentlessly counting my steps, one, two, three, and a half steps, turn around and repeat it again and again and again. It was a kind of self-torture. Now I knew what the wild animals in the zoo were going through. Pacing was comforting, expelling of energy bursting to get out and at the same time cursing myself for being here, "thank God I'm alone" I thought. "What do you want! I yelled", breaking the spell, "I told you No! Go away!" I said, "I'll burn you! Burn you like I've always done". I tried to narrow my focus and restrain my imagination, but it got worse. I thought I was losing it.

Then the flood began. I got a rush of thoughts going through my head with a buzzing volume and force of a speeding train. I thought I was going insane. I thought this stuff only happens in the movies, but here it was happening to me. I knew it was God or a Spirit or an Angel talking to me. Still I refused in my stubbornness, an area where I thought I was king. It got quiet again for a moment, a calm, warm silence, and then I heard it. It was in my head, heart, I couldn't tell and I could see her, my daughter, downstairs in the visiting room booth. She was standing on the shelf, banging on the glass window yelling, "Ta-Ta! Open up! Ta-Ta open up!"…

All in a moment, I knew, and the scripture came to me, "that out of the mouths of babes, you will hear the word of God"…I no longer had the power to refuse. "O.K.! O.K.!" I said, " I'm yours, what do you want me to do?" I said…

In the same moment, a sense of emotion welled in my eyes. It was very different and I could feel again. My God, I was feeling, really feeling and I was glad to let it flow. My heart seemed to melt away. From the top of my head, a warmness down through my body like tingling and with it, a very heavy weight or burden being lifted off my chest from the root of my soul. Tears flowed free for the first time since I was a child, kidnapped, molested and traumatized. Never truly feeling until this moment of relief and revelation. It was like being alive again. I was alive! I was dead and I was alive again! A sense of peace from the agony I have been enduring was present. I know I must have literally, been glowing in the dark radiating an Inner Light. It was a darkness I carried for almost twenty-seven years and this moment was the relief from the bonds of pain I had endured for so long…It was like, being born again.

*   *   *

I didn't know how much time had transpired and at the time, frankly, I didn't really care about time, I was feeling good! Wow, feel, to be able to truly feel again. It was a new experience and now I realized why, I was so cold, quiet and I never cried at funerals, movies, weddings, or the birth of a child or where I was supposed too. When I would see someone feeling low, I couldn't relate to it nor have any empathy what so ever. It's really hard to explain an experience like that, but now I had hope and no matter what happened, I was free. Even though in prison, free of the life I had created for myself; free of the fears I carried with me since childhood. I knew I had a long way to go and change would be slow and I had some very serious matters ahead of me.

Life is funny, not funny Ha! Ha! but, funny weird. The following story could be you, or your son or daughter. It could happen to anyone, rich or poor, black, white, red, brown or yellow or green. My only hope is that it brings light, where there is darkness. That there is a way to change and heal the old wounds. This story is a view from the side of the survivor. It also is a view of the product of child predators and racial tensions. How a severe trauma created an avenue over time and pain for escape through drug addiction and self-destructive behavior. Also how an early traumatic experience could change the entire life of a victim. The times did not have the assistance of today and even today, the public is unaware of the atrocities we bear. There is a way to prevent ourselves from self-destruction and we addicts are not doomed. The courage starts with our willingness to live normally and this normality can give our emotional, physical, intellectual and spiritual selves' back again to becoming a whole person. These are the gifts I took for granted which I'll share them with you. This book takes place over four decades each decade has its cultural identity along with its ironies of the times we live. It also has a future and a hope for all, especially if you were once a victim of the misgivings of society or with similar circumstances.

I have always wondered, "Why am I still alive?" Perhaps, to write this book and share with you why any of us are, and give you a sense of strength, courage, hope and the desire to seek out a better self.

The 50's

(The Changeling)

◆

I was born a Baby Boomer. A child of the Atomic Age, August 1950, in Orange California at the Chapman General Hospital—now UCI Medical Center. The hospital was the biggest thing then and quite the latest in technology. Later, I was to return with scarlet fever.

My memories are fragmented. It's a wonder I still have any memories left or a brain for that matter. There was a time at age two, I could remember when we, my brothers and sister, were playing in a field on Monrovia and Superior streets in Costa Mesa. We lived on a hill overlooking the ocean just off the coast highway. My aunt Judy was carrying me through a barbed wire fence, across a field of cows, where the grass was tall and into the middle of three huge oil storage tanks, where we could hide from the rest until we were found. Hide n' seek, tag your it. It was a beautiful place overlooking the ocean and I can remember the sunsets, bright orange and purple etched into my mind, as the sun would dip into the ocean. The sparkling waters like dancing stars slowly turning colors into the evening. This I could see from the window facing the ocean and it will always stay with me. That's the earliest recollection I have. Sometimes I question if I imagined it. Could I have made it up? We did live there, the field, the tanks, the cows, although now gone in fact, they were there.

In the field, my father would plant crops overlooking the ocean. It was heaven and some of the crops would be sold at my grandfathers market on Fifth Street in Santa Ana. My grandmother would mind the store and my grandfather would sell fruits and vegetables from a truck to all the different *barrios* in Orange County. Back then the county seemed bigger because it was harder to get from one place to another with many dirt roads. Later I was to go with my grandfather on his routes.

At this time, I had two older brothers and a sister. My oldest brother was Michael, next came Manuel, who we called Monnie. My older sister, Cathy was more my age so we were close. There was one time during a rain and my brothers were coming home from school. They were taking a short cut to get out of the rain when Michael stepped into, and got stuck in mire. This was soggy soil mixed with crude oil much like a tar pit. With water on top, it looks like a small pool of water, but can be very deadly. With no one around, Monnie pulled on Michael's arm as hard as he could, but could not get Michael out. No matter how hard he tried, the suction from the crude oil held Michael in. Monnie couldn't let go to go for help or Michael would sink. Scared, cold, tired and wet, they both started yelling for help and none came. This area was far away from anyone and avoided by those who knew of the crude pits. Realizing that nobody was going to come to help, it was up to Monnie to get Michael out. With all his strength he pulled and told Michael to give it all he had as they both made a last ditch effort. With all the strength they could muster, Monnie pulled and pulled at Michael and Michael tried to ease himself up. Slowly, Michael started to come free and it took all the energy they had to do it. Both boys laid there, exhausted, in the rain, covered in oil and mud, happy to be alive. They were just trying to get home from school, and they never told mom.

Those were times when you could drink water from the tap and it was sweet, clean, fresh tasting. The air was clean and the dirt from the roads gave it a country look. As kids, we found anything we could to make toys with, even if it was just a plank of wood or a discarded old roller skate. My Dad was good with building materials and made toys for my brothers. His ideas did inspire others. We didn't know we were poor and my parents worked hard to make sure we got enough to eat. They always worked hard and believed in big families as we had another sister on the way.

About three years later we moved. We lived in a small two-bedroom house on the corner of Fourth Street and Forrest in Santa Ana. It was a corner house and across the street was Russ' Saw Shop and next door was a Baptist Church. I always thought that church was great because I liked the singing and stomping that went on in there during the week-nights. If people ever had the Holy Ghost, it was they. The ladies from the church were extremely nice, especially when they brought us sweet potato pie, which is still is a favorite. Across the street in front of us was Franklin elementary school where I would eventually attend kinder-garten. That house was old, but it had many memories to it, like the first time we got a television that I recall. This was the 50's and we were poor, so the first television we got didn't have any sound. Not that there was no sound in those days, but it was all we could afford. I got to watch, "Mighty Joe Young" about a giant ape, like "King Kong". For us kids, this was excitement and we were thrilled at this new technology. My dad did get the television repaired and one of my favorite shows was "Al Jarvis" and the "bunny-hop". To this day, I haven't found anyone who remem-bers him and sometimes I think he might have been my imagination, but I sure liked the dancing and songs.

By this time we had a little sister, Christine, and little did we know that although we couldn't hear the television, she would never be able to hear it. Christine was special and was born in Mexico while my mother was visiting there. She had complications and was born premature. She was kept in a hospital until my mother arranged to take her home. She was so small, my parents said she could fit in the palm of your hand and needed better care than was possible in Mexico. They brought her in a basket lined with hot water bottles. Kind of a home made incubator back to the United States along the old back roads. My mother said, "it was one of the longest worrisome rides she ever had taken".

This was a time when my dad had his own gardening service and my mom worked as a cashier at "Buds" produce stand off Main and Sunflower which bordered Costa Mesa. Both my parents speak English and were born here in the United States. They also speak Spanish, but never really forced it on us. My grandparents from my mother's side both speak English and were born here. My grandfather Charles is from Texas. Although Charles was the Grandfather I grew up with, I had a biological grandfather of which I never knew until my mother read part of this book. He was full-blooded Irishman by the name of Edward Walten who died of a ruptured appendix. My grandmother Catherine is from Santa Barbara. She is our Native American side and a Chumash Indian. These are mission Indians from the Santa Barbara coast and Channel Islands. My grandfather, Martin from my dads side was orphaned and from Durango, Mexico and was adopted by the Morales family. I understand that his original last name was Garay. My grandmother on my dad's side is Maria. The Torres family is widespread and we have many beloved family members like my *Tio* Paolo and my Tia Antonia. My dad's side of the family speaks little English except his brothers and sisters, so we had to learn Spanish in order to communicate. It was funny at times cause us kids spoke broken Spanish and our grandparents broken English. It made for some interesting gestures and name calling like, *mocoso*, *pocho*, *pendejo* and *burro*. At the same time other family members would try to get us kids to speak Spanish, but the importance of it just didn't seem to sink in at the time.

My little sister Christine was older now and all she wanted to do was play and had endless amounts of energy. When she was born prematurely, she had more complications at the hospital where I was born and was disfigured when the oxygen tube was placed in her nose and left there. The plastics used in those days created an allergic reaction, which caused degeneration to her skin tissue. My mother suspected something was wrong and ever so slowly lifted the soft cotton swab covering her nose. She was shocked to discover as a result of the plastic; the left part of her nostril came off. She suffered some brain damage and lost her hearing ability. Now that she was a bit older, Christine was fine, so long as we were playing, but once in the house, she would break any and everything she could get her hands on. It made for some very interesting situations in our household.

Christine and I were outside a lot and sometimes we would sneak away or rather I would sneak her away with me. One summer day when both my parents were away at work, I took Christine with me and snuck away from the babysitter. I remembered this place where they had fish in the back yard and we were going to catch some for dinner. We headed across the trolley car tracks on Fourth Street, over towards Third Street next to a lumber yard, where I had seen the fish from their neighbors back fence. They were compadres of my dad. When we got there, nobody was home, so we went around the side to the back yard and there it was. A beautiful pond, looking like a jungle and what kid could resist. I was a kid of five years and Chrisy was three. I tried various methods to get the fish and my clumsy attempts failed. Chrisy was having fun and got all wet and so did I. Feet wet, clothes wet and the heat of the day made it all an adventure and fun. I looked over to the patio area, the lady that lived there had some old pots and pans and I had an idea. I started bailing the water out of the pond. While I bailed, Chrisy splashed and what a mess we made, water everywhere. As I got closer to catching the fish by hand, the faster I bailed. They were large golden carp, beautiful, majestic and I couldn't wait to get them into a frying pan. Time past and we were there hours before I knew it. I got a few fish in a pan and off we went home. When I got there with Chrisy and the fish, the babysitter was yelling and fussing and I couldn't tell what she was saying, just that she was mad. I caught a few words like, *Mama*, *Papa* and *nino pendejo*. She took Chrisy and cleaned her up and I was in the kitchen, getting the fish ready to fry or trying to when mom came home. I thought I was going to make her proud of me and I was excited to show her what I had done.

I ended up in our room. The babysitter had called mom at work and mom was mad that she had to leave work, but also worried sick about us kids. She or my dad never hit or spanked me, but I know she wanted too. Still to this day, she reminds me of the scare I gave her, and the fear of losing Chrisy. Chrisy was special, and mom knew, that sooner or later Chrisy was going to hurt herself or one of us kids. She had a habit of running into the street and she was fast. I couldn't see the difference, so long as we were together and outside, she was fine.

I always thought it was my fault when Chrisy finally had to go away. It was 1955 and a really great time, at least until Chrisy had to go away to a hospital in Pomona and we visited almost every weekend. All of us kids would be packed up with a lunch for the ride to Pomona. My favorite songs were "Yakety-Yak" and "Charlie Brown". Dad turned up the radio and I would sing and act as we rolled along. It was a hard time for dad and mom. To chose between your kids, when all the attention had to go to one and not the others. This way Chrisy could get close attention and her first year away was difficult to adjust to, but she eventually did well enough to take care of herself. Being a kid, I could always remember there was sadness when the subject of Chrisy came up, but being a kid, it was always a feeling quickly put away.

This was about the time our sixth member of the family came home; we had a little brother, Mark. On the day my parents brought him home, somebody yelled "they're coming!" and I ran outside to see our old car pulling up in the dirt driveway. Before my dad could park, we were hanging on the door to see mom holding this little bundle in her arms. My sister Cathy and I kept jumping up and down with eyes wide open and everybody was happy. We got visitors for days afterward and they would bring treats for us kids.

When I was to start kindergarten, the school was right across the street. It was easy to get there and I could come right home with no hassles. This was Franklin Elementary and like a kid I couldn't wait for the first day at school, I was so excited. Back in 1955-56, a person could go the Broadway Theatre for twenty cents and on the corner of Fourth Street and Broadway was Pringles Drug store. Here, you could get a triple-decker ice cream cone for a dime and buy a Snickers bar, an Abba-Zaba, and an Almond Joy for a dime. On Main Street, just around the corner was the West Coast Theater owned by Mr. Edwards. If you went on your birthday, you would get a free giant "Sugar Daddy" candy bar that weighed about a two pounds. This thing was so big; it took days to finish. I was totally surprised when they called my name for my birthday. My brother Monnie took me and told them it was my birthday. There also was the State Theatre on Fourth Street where I saw my first scary pictures; the "Tarantula" and "IT Came From Outer Space". I had nightmares but it was a treat just to be able to go to the show. I gathered many a pop bottle to earn money for the weekends and get somebody to take me.

There was something about going downtown, it was exciting and Santa Ana was small then but wonderful to be in. We were used to the *barrios* staying with friends and relatives. I used to go with my grandfather on his runs to different *barrios* like here in *Artesia, Santa Nita, Silver Acres, Logan* and *El Modena,* selling fruits and vegetables from his old 1929 Ford converted pick-up truck. It had a catering shell on the back and the sides that open up and the racks of fruit were beautifully displayed. My grandfather was an easygoing person with many stories to tell. His stories were always virtuous and taught you a lesson you might need later in life. He had a wooden leg, lost from a carriage accident when his horse bolted and his leg was caught in the spokes. It was difficult to drive the truck with his wooden leg and my dad, who was really good at creating engineering feats, made a cross member piece of material that connected the brake and the clutch. This enabled my grandfather to change gears when he would have to slow down by just pressing the clutch/brake. He knew the kids in the barrios would run up behind the truck, reach their hand in and grab a snack from the back. It was always open and when the ladies would come out smiling, giving salutations saying, "*buenos Dias Don Martin, Que tenemos en especial?*" I saw times when he would count and say in Spanish, five cents for this or three cents for that and five cents for that tomato under your apron. The lady would blush and say, "*perdoname Don Martin*" and before she could explain, he would smile and say in Spanish, "that's O.K. you can pay me when you get the money". He was very kind to people and everyone loved him. I'd think sometimes, my grandpa was the only one people could depend on to get a decent meal when money was scarce. This is not to imply that Mexicans are thieves, but these were hard times and many of the families were migrant workers following the picking seasons. My grandfather was there for them when they needed it. Random acts of kindness built a very strong character and respect for my grandfather. At the end of the day, we headed home and unloaded what was left on the truck to get it ready for the next days produce shopping. He would give me a dollar for a whole days work and that was a lot of money for me cause all I had to do was ring the bell and watch for people coming out at the favorite stops.

My grandmother, Maria passed away when I was very young, about four or five years old. She was robust and very caring, hardworking and took a strict interest in us kids. She would be up at 3 a.m. to make grandfather's *café con leche* and have a *pan de semita* ready for him. Grandfather would leave for Los Angeles at 3:30 a.m. to pick up the day's fruits and vegetables. At 7:00 a.m. grandmother would walk every day to the family store with her little mutt dog, who only knew Spanish, to open the store. When you're around grandma, you behaved or else, and she always had a bunch of grandkids around the house, especially during the summertime. When she passed away, my uncle Manuel found her on the back door steps next to the cage where she kept her canaries she loved so much. Her birds were always treated special and she had a golden touch when it came to birds. The reason is she was able to breed them in captivity and in those days, to do that was special. The last time I saw her, she was in a casket at Brown's Mortuary on Seventeenth Street in Santa Ana. My Uncle Felix saw me in the crowd of family mourners and picked me up, so I could look in the casket. My grandma lay there, motionless and although this was my first experience of death, I felt the crowd around me and I knew it was bad for them. I also knew that she didn't have to worry, because I could feel a sense of peace around her and she looked like she was just asleep. Everyone around me reassured me she had gone to heaven, and as I grew older, I would get to know her even better from the stories my relatives would tell. One of the stories was with my brothers, my sister and a few cousins. I scared my mom and my grandma playing baseball one day in the back yard. Although I was too young to play baseball, I was in the area playing in the dirt collecting pieces of wood, rocks and the like when I walked in the area of home plate. Well, from what I heard, I managed to run into the bat at full swing and I got clobbered right in the forehead. It got suddenly real quiet outside. When mom and grandma heard nothing but silence, they came out and found me lying in a pool of blood and there wasn't a kid in sight. There were lots of hiding places and when the rest of the kids were rounded up, surprisingly, nobody knew what happened.

This was Fairlawn Street, famous to the Mexican community right in the middle of the *Artesia Barrio*. When the family kids got together, we took up the whole street in front of grandpa's house to play what we called "*Mexican circle*". All the families would meet at grandpas' for Christmas and he would have gifts for all kids who came and there was an endless supply of *tamales, pan dulce, atole',* and *menudo.* In a glass bowl filled to the brim at the end of the living room, were candy canes. Sometimes it was a test for the children, to see if they would respectfully greet Grandpa and Grandma upon entering, instead of running right passed and to the candy bowl. Just to give you an idea of how big the family is, I had 35 first cousins not including any of their children. The numbers changed as time goes by.

Just before we moved from the Fourth Street house, my father bought me a brand new Schwinn bicycle and I remember trying to prove that I could ride it. After practicing on my own for a time and felt assured, I could ride it alone. I ran inside to call my dad and mom, excited of my newfound experience and I couldn't wait to show them. Once outside and I got their attention, I put my foot on the pedal and pushed off. For some reason I kept pushing and pushing, going in circles, but I just couldn't get on the bike. As I was going in circles, I could see that my dad and mom were getting short on patience and probably thinking I was cute. They went inside and no sooner than they did; I got on the bike riding like a pro only no one to watch. I never blamed them, but it did stay on my mind.

It was about half way through the year 1956 when my parents bought a home in the southwest part of Santa Ana. I say half way, because it was half way through the first grade and it was my last year at Franklin Elementary. My new school was called Monte Vista. The new house was two years old and although I didn't notice it, it was in an all white neighborhood and I was soon to find out that I was not Mexican American but a Mexican. The house was huge, compared to where we had just come from and across the street was an orange grove with lots of places to play and hide. This was a four bedroom, two-bath house and it had a big back yard and patio and since it was a corner lot, there was plenty of room to play baseball on the side street. The area was covered with many orange groves then, and I used them as markers to find my way home from school. At this time, Westeria was a dead end at Shelly Street. From there, it was an orange grove to Sullivan Street. Looking west from the new house, the dead end Street was marked with large diamond pattern signs with reflectors in them. To me, that was my street and my house was four streets and a long block from there. Heading toward the dead end, I could turn left on Raitt Street, one block to Monte Vista, turn right to the school. Two turns, that's all I had to do. Well, the first day of my new school, I was trying to remember that all day after I was dropped off. After school on my way home, I went back the same way, made a left on Raitt towards my street. When I got to my street and looked both ways, I didn't see any diamond shaped signs. I felt a big lump in my throat and went further ahead to the next street, which was Myrtle. I knew it seemed too far and started to get scared. I backtracked to my street again, and again looked both ways. No signs, but I went towards the dead end and found out that construction crews had removed the signs to make a road through to Sullivan Street. I went back the other way and eventually found the new house. I remember it because I was scared and lost. I was sure glad to be home. For a six and a half-year-old, this was traumatic for me, but little did I know what trauma is.

At this time, the school was still a new project, in that it was desegregated. I thought all schools were like that, and I had no idea what desegregation was. At first, school was great and I made new friends. I met this kid who was a neighbor just three houses down from me and we played often after school. One day we were playing at his house in the front yard, when his dad came home. He didn't say "Hi," nothing. He just looked at us and told his son, "get in the house". I went home feeling puzzled, it was too early to go in, "maybe they had to go somewhere", I thought. The next day I went to his house and knocked on the door. When he answered, his dad was standing right behind him and I asked if he could come out and play. He said, "no, I can't", with his eyes looking down. His dad would nudge him from behind, like wanting him to say something else. I said, "O K!" and with my head down, turned to walk away. The next thing I knew, I was hit from behind in the back of my head, knocking me down with a big rock about the size of softball. The back of my head was bleeding and I struggled to get up and run away. Looking back, I could see my friend shaking and in tears. So was I, as I ran home a few doors down. I guess my parents thought it was an accident and nothing ever came of it, which I could remember. I never realized it and was naive of any racial hatred. Years later after looking back, then I knew, that we were the only Mexican Americans being viewed as Mexicans in an all white neighborhood. I know this sounds harsh and I wish it never happened, but it did. I still have that scar. I also learned, that we are taught hatred.

There were other incidents, like when I was in school and I saw most of the kids had brown bag lunches. Nice, newly folded bags or brand new metal lunch boxes with Roy Rogers or the Lone Ranger on them. All I had was the plastic bag from an empty loaf of Weber's Bread. You could see the bean burrito wrapped in wax paper inside, right through the plastic bag. I tried to hide it out of shame from the looks I got and the laughter that it created. I would come home and ask my mom, "What's a *braserro*?" or "what's a *wet back*?" or "what's a *beaner*?" I was so dumb, I couldn't tell when I was insulted or I refused to believe that it happened.

My mom would take us kids shopping with her at the "A & P" grocery store on the corner of McFadden and Bristol. My mother is a very light skinned person and looks white or should I say Caucasian. A lady at the store asked her in a gruff tone, "what are you doing with all these Mexican kids?" Mom said, "I beg your pardon! These are my kids". Mom stood up for us and at the time all I knew was that mom was mad at the lady, but didn't know why or that we had been insulted. It was a changing time for this neighborhood and I didn't realize I was part of the changes that were to come. Although I made more friends and we played in the orchards after school, everything seemed to be going well. People were nice and all, but the "For Sale" signs started going up all over the place, and in the neighborhoods by my school too. It took a couple of years and the change was subtle, but more Mexican and Black families started to move in as the White families were moving out.

A year later I was going to catechism to study for my first communion. This is a Catholic rite for children to accept the body and blood of

Jesus Christ in receiving the host at mass on Sunday. I studied my prayers, believed in Jesus and did well. I thought everything was going to be fine. The day of my first communion was an exciting time for me having made it through all the schooling. I was all dressed up in new clothes my mom and nina bought just like the other kids. I was excited and ready to go into church to start the ceremony when my mom called me aside and said,

"Mijo, I'm sorry but you won't be able to make your first communion today".

She looked upset and I was shocked.

"But why mom?" I asked.

"Because we didn't bring your baptismal record and we couldn't find it."

"Mijo, we tried everything", my godmother added.

I didn't know that mom and my *nina*, had gone to *San Ysidro* where I was baptized to get a copy, but the church had since burned down and no record could be found in the surrounding churches. I know now how hard it must have been for my mother and Godmother to tell me. I was heartbroken and confused. I couldn't understand why God needed a piece of paper to make my first communion. I thought this was from the heart and felt like I wasn't wanted and was slowly losing my mind.

We did stay for the mass and when it was time to go up and receive the host, I would just sit in the pew and cry as I watched all the others in my group go up before me. If ever I had a broken heart, it was then. I sat in the pew fuming at God, mad at him, mad at Jesus. A child, failing to see that it was not God, but man, who made the rule.

*   *   *

I was just finishing the fourth grade and nine years old and I had a friend named Larry who lived across the street from the school. In fact, you can see the school from his back yard. We often played at the park behind the school after baseball practice. On Saturdays, we would go to the "Holiday Lanes" bowling alley on First Street to play pinball machines. Larry was hard of hearing in one ear and couldn't hear out of the other. Larry was a little slower than the rest of the kids and I often helped him with his homework and he often helped me with my chores at home. Larry's parents were nice people and always invited me in to eat, where we would do our homework on the kitchen table. One day, after we finished our homework, we went to the bowling alley to play games. Now, sometimes when we were playing, and I knew how much money he had and he knew how much money I had, but Larry always came up with extra money to play with. This time, I knew how much we started out with and when it was gone, Larry came up with more money.

"Where did you get the money Larry?" I asked him.

"I got it from my uncle" he said.

Although I didn't know who or what his uncle looked like, I looked around to see if I could spot who he was. Larry gave me enough for a couple more games. I played for awhile on one machine and he was further down the alley playing his favorite machine. I was lost in my game when Larry and this man approached me.

"This is my uncle", and told his uncle, "this is my friend Mario".

"Hi!" I said

He asked me my last name. I told him it was, Morales, and continued to play the machine. He made small talk for awhile and every now and then would give me a quarter for the machine. I kept looking around for Larry, but he was nowhere in sight and I was starting to get a bad feeling about this. I asked his uncle, if he knew where Larry was and he said, he saw him go outside. "Just like Larry", I thought to myself.

"Do you want to go outside and look for him?" he asked in a heavy Spanish accent. I don't know why I did, but the next decision I made, I would regret for the rest of my life. I went with him towards the outside door and at the same time wanted to know where Larry was. I wasn't feeling very comfortable with this guy. He put his hand on my shoulder and we walked out. Little did I know that I had just played into the hands of the devil. This man lied to me and told me that Larry had gone home and he coaxed me to his car by offering a ride to Larry's house. I was getting really scared now and couldn't believe this was happening and that at any moment, Larry would show up and it would be all right. We got closer to his car and I kept looking around wondering if I should trust this guy or not. He opened the door on the right side and told me to get in the back seat cause the front seat didn't work right and like a dumb little kid, I did. When he went around to open the door on his side, instead of getting in the driver's seat, he got into the back seat with me. I think that's when my world began to cave in and I went into shock, shear terror and couldn't find it in myself to scream or yell. I sat there like the scared rabbit in the road with the car headlights on it not moving. He sexually molested me and I kept saying to myself, Larry, where are you? Why did you do this to me! This is not happening. I tried to fight, but his hand held the back of my neck as I tried to resist. I was crying and wanted out of this nightmare cause I thought he was going to kill me and dump me in an orange grove.

He didn't, and gave me a couple of bucks opened the door and told me, "you tell no one or I will come after you" or something of the same meaning. I ran hard and fast, I never ran so hard in my life and as I ran towards Larry's house, I kept thinking, "I should have bit it off," then I probably would really be dead. I kept looking back to see if he was following, scared that he might just come after me. Scared at what my parent's would do for being so stupid. Shamed for them and feeling shame for myself. As I ran, I felt like my whole life was catching up to me in a bad dream, sweating and my heart pounding, gasping for air as I ran. I didn't know I was suffering a trauma or the first effects of it. I didn't even know what a trauma was. All I knew is that I was scared and kept running.

Larry's house was about a mile away and when I got there I vomited in his yard. I was sick to my stomach and gasping for air. I knocked on the door hoping Larry was there. Larry opened the door and came out.

"You butthole!" I shouted, glad to see he was all right and mad at him for getting me into this situation.

"Do you know what your uncle did?" I grabbed the garden hose started to wash the vomit on the grass and rinse my mouth with water. Larry's mom came out to see what the yelling was about. I told her what happened.

Larry said, "that man wasn't my uncle, I just said that". Larry said it just like that dumb kid "Larry" on the TV "Leave it to Beaver Show". Larry's mom called the cops. All I could think was, How could you lie like that Larry. Larry was known to tell a few lies before or to be a fibber, but this, why?

*   *   *

When the police came, a detective also came and asked a lot of questions. I told them what I knew and so did Larry. I remember the detective asking me, "did he molest you in a sexual way"?

"Yes", I said, crying at the shame I felt and the fear of anyone knowing what happened.

"Could you recognize this guy?

"Yes."

"Would you be willing to go see if he was still there and could you identify him?

I hesitated, and I thought to myself, "I wish he was dead".

"Yes."

The detective took me in an unmarked police car back to the Holiday Lanes and Larry's mom was trying to get hold of my parents. Once at the bowling alley, the detective had me wait outside with a uniformed police officer while he went in to check the description I had given. He came back and said,

"I think he's in there. There's a man on the west wall, sitting next to the pool table waiting his turn, that fits your description".

I was scared and my heart was pumping hard and I felt like I was going to be sick.

"You'll be alright. All you have to do is point him out and don't let him see you. I'll be right next to you," said the detective.

I went in and a divider wall was perfect for cover. Sure enough, he was there. I hated him and he was stupid enough to stay there. I pointed at him whispering, "that's him right there." From that point, the uniformed officer led me outside, and the detective went in to make his arrest.

I thought it was over, but they wanted me to go to the police station and point him out again. I was afraid the man would see me, but was assured by the detective that there was a one way glass mirror. The room was dark as I was led in and I wanted to vomit. I could see the man through the glass window.

I did what they said and learned he had been arrested for kidnapping and child molestation; in addition, he had other charges of which I can't remember. The whole thing was a nightmare from the beginning. I felt sick to my gut and I don't know what I was feeling, but I know I was afraid of everything.

When I finally got home in a police car, I couldn't look my mom or dad in the eye. My mom was crying from worry and my dad was his usual stern self.

"You don't talk about this, this is something you don't talk about, understand?"

None of my brothers or sisters was there to see this. That's the way it was in those days. My parents meant well and they raised us well, but those words stayed with me.

It took a few days and I was starting to feel really low and confused. I was in my own little world and was misinterpreting what everyone was saying. Although Larry promised not to tell any kids at school, I couldn't trust him anymore. I felt paranoid, that they knew what happened and when they laughed, I thought they were laughing at me. I didn't realize it then, but this man had stolen my dreams, my goals, and my future. I wouldn't find this out for another thirty years.

I was kidnapped, molested and in the following year, I slit my wrist. It was like an omen of self-destruction. I felt God rejected me. To this day, I think my family thought I did it on purpose, but it was an accident. All the kids in school had safety training and became more safety conscious around school and at home. At the time, my brother Michael worked as a box-boy at a local market. In my room, he left his box cutter on the window ledge. It's a flattened metal jacket with a single edge razor that slides in and out. Well this one was left open and I thought it was dangerous and could cut someone, so I tried to close it. As I pulled on it, the razor edge was pointing toward my wrist and when it finally gave way, it went right down the center of my forearm. Today, it's about a four and a half- inch scar, but to me then, it was half way up my arm. This was not going across the wrist, but the long way. At first, I didn't even notice it until the blood started to flow, then I got scared and yelled. My dad came and put pressure on it, made me hold my arm up and went for some first aid. We had no insurance, so my dad did what he could. He opened the wound and poured alcohol generously into it and I screamed at the pain. He then started cutting strips of tape and placed them equally along the cut to close it. It worked better than stitches, but I didn't find that out till years later.

My world was starting to change and I couldn't smile at life anymore. I was slowly becoming a different person, starting to withdraw and travel a lonely path that was a living hell. I was feeling sorry for myself and that was dangerous, because once you start, it's hard to stop. I couldn't recognize what I was doing to myself. I got to a point where it became a self-loathing and pity. The sad part is that I came to like it. I was miserable and I couldn't understand the feelings or what was happening to me. I thought I was the only one in the world that this could happen to, and I had nowhere to turn. Worse of all, no one to turn to that I could trust. I slowly learned how to mask my feelings and cover them up like an invisible coat of armor. Instead of building and developing character, I was hiding it, not wanting anyone to discover my secret. I went from one extreme to the other. I couldn't solve problems so I was getting into fights at school. Instead of voicing my feelings, I held them in until I couldn't stand it anymore. I let it out by being the hero who would fight the big kid that was picking on the little ones. I got my butt kicked a few times and either way, if I won or lost I was still the hero. Being the hero made me feel good, it lifted me up, but it was temporary. On the other hand, I played baseball in little league both at El Salvador and Jerome Park. I liked baseball because I could hide well from my feelings. Baseball was always the focal point and when we won, I felt part of the team spirit. That too was temporary. Meanwhile, I was alone.

My sister Cathy took me to games or I went with her when she had something to do. My mother had told her to watch me and take care of me, and she resented the fact that she always had to take care of me. Never knowing what had happened or why she had to. At age 11, I started smoking cigarettes. I stole a pack of Pall Mall's from my aunt, and went by myself where nobody could see, next to the ditch that ran along side of Jerome Park. The first puff I successfully got into my lungs, I got high. A little dizzy, slightly nauseous feeling, but for the first time in what seemed my life, I got away from the pain and fear for a moment. This was just another secret I began to bear. I couldn't understand what I was feeling only it was just a little bit better than before.

At this time I had a friend named Tommy. He lived close to the school and close to my house and would come over often. One day he came over to help me. He had just gotten a pair of new tennis shoes. While we were out in the yard and I was mowing the lawn, I ran over his new tennis shoes. Thank God, I didn't take his toes with it because my dad had a heavy-duty lawn mower. Either I was careless or I did it intentionally. Somehow, I may have been trying to scare him.

I kept going from one extreme to the other. I would do well in school, yet one time Tommy and I ran away from home for three days and stayed in a hayloft at Lukens Dairy on the corner of Raitt and Edinger. Both Tommy and I were easily led and when the ideas came up to do something wrong neither one of us was strong enough to say no! At school I was fine. I square danced, I won a mashed potato dancing contest, was in a talent show contest. This was with two friends Joe and Ray. Joe liked to sing and had many 45 records of doo-wop, rhythm and blues and rock n" roll. We were on the stage singing to the Duke of Earl from a record player in front of the whole auditorium full of kids.

I was on the school safety patrol and was a crossing guard with a red sweater, badge, yellow cap and a red staff. This was a program sponsored by the Santa Ana Police Department and worked well if you could hang on to your staff. The kids from Smedley Junior High and Valley High would walk by the crossing going home from school and take the staffs away. I never lost mine and I was either lucky or it was my size that kept the troublemakers away. I had two white girlfriends who liked to sneak into the orange grove across from the school to smoke cigarettes. But two guy friends of mine said I shouldn't be hanging around with white people.

"They'll get you in trouble", Joe used to say. My friend Ray went along with everything Joe would say.

One day, at Ray's house, Ray's dad gave us boxing gloves and told us to spar in his garage and he'd be the referee. At this time I hadn't realized how big I was getting, nor did I realize my own strength. No matter how much I refused, Ray's dad insisted I box with Ray. The spar lasted about two seconds when I hit Ray with an uppercut and he literally went up off his feet and landed on his butt. I felt like a big dummy and at the same time exhilarated. It scared me, because although I have been in a few fights, I never liked them. The gloves seemed safe enough and we stayed friends. At least until we started to have differences of opinion. According to Joe and Ray, we were Mexicans and being Mexicans we were supposed to dress in khakis and wear J.C.Penny's Towncraft tee shirts and keep our shoes shined so you can see your face in the tip.

Well, yea! That was cool, but they also said, we shouldn't have any *gaba-cho* friends or girl friends, which I had at the time. I dressed like them right after a baseball game and out of uniform.

I broke up with my girlfriend. I chose to break up with her and I remember her asking, why?

"Because your white", I said.

It was too late. It came out of my mouth and in what seemed like harmless remarks, I had become a racist. It was then that I realized how much it hurt. It hurt her and it hurt me and I knew I was wrong. I was encapsulating myself in someone else's world, a world I would struggle to get out of for a long time.

Had it not been for the friends like Joe and Ray keeping me busy, I think I would have gone crazy. I was all right with them, but when I was alone or at home, I was different. I always carried this certain sort of sadness about me, like a dark cloud hanging over my head. When I would walk home alone from the park through the halls of the school, I felt like I was the only person in the world. I found myself wishing someone would come and save me, someone who knew what I was going through. Someone who could recognize my troubles when I walked with my head down, my silent cry for help. It became a behavior pattern with me for other people to carry the conversation and my social skills were…well I didn't have any, unless I was asked a direct question. I thought I was a psychological moron or that I had serious psychological problems, that's the best way to place this memory. I did ask questions, but what I did ask appeared boring to others. So subjects like the moon and stars, animals and everyday things we take for granted became my interest because they couldn't talk back.

I remember also when the subject of girls and sex came up, I tried to avoid it and became paranoid. This area was getting to close to my secret, my fear of anyone knowing what had happened and the fear of becoming ridiculed. Not only that, I was afraid that whoever ridiculed me for that purpose would get terribly hurt cause it was just a fuse waiting to be lit. I had become a changed person and the changes just kept coming as I tried my best to hide and blend in with the people I thought were normal.

Thr 60'S
(The Trap Door)

◆

It was the year 1962 and we now had a new addition to the family, a little sister named Monica. She was a beautiful child and kept mom busy and dad was gleaming with his new queen. I thank God for my new sister because she had a way of taking away the pain just being around her. That's when I was home, but outside I was a twelve-year-old looking for acceptance and getting into trouble. I still went to church, but my attitude was that the church didn't want me, so I didn't want it. I stayed for services because both my parents wanted it so. It was painful when the time came to go up to the altar and receive the host. I just sat in the pew and was heartbroken knowing that I couldn't because I had not made my first communion, nor had I ever gone to confession. I was becoming a spiritual and emotional mess and was always confused. This confusion eventually crept into every thought process I had or when any form of stress started to take place.

By this time my parents were worried about me. I had gotten into trouble hanging out and vandalizing what we called a haunted house just down the street. It was abandoned with broken windows and holes in it all over the place. It must have been built in the Twenties, had two stories and the A frame roof was caving in with green mold where the trees touched the roof. In the back, it had a garage with a living area attached, like a small apartment. To the left of the house was a giant oak, which we called a hanging tree, because it looked spooky. We did break a few windows, but mainly we were trying to catch pigeons living in the attic. This house had some feather foot, tumbler pigeons, which were a prize and would add to my collection. We added a few more holes to the roof and I was sent to juvenile hall for it.

I only spent a week in juvenile hall with three days in isolation confinement. Even in isolation, I wanted a cigarette and the guy next to me said, "I heard you can smoke lettuce". Like a dummy, I saved my lettuce from my dinner tray, dried it out, and rolled it in some magazine paper. I managed to get a light and smoked the lettuce. I gagged and everyone in the unit got a big laugh! It took me awhile before I could also laugh at being so stupid. I didn't like it there, but the food was good and the cook lived right across the street from us, so he took care of me. I was put on probation for a few years.

I met Nick from Seventh Street and he was a party person and seemed to know where all the parties were in the *Artesia Barrio*. We drank wine on the weekends and I would sneak out at night and go to parties on Seventh Street or Holly Street. In someone's garage, listening to 45's of "Oldies but Goodies" on the record player and couples would be slow dancing with a little blue light hanging in the middle of the garage. We always ended up outside the liquor store trying to get someone to buy us a bottle of Thunderbird wine. Trying to get home was the trick for me cause at twelve-thirty in the morning, it's easy to spot a kid walking, so I had a few fleeing moments from the police. The police spotted me on Fifth and Raitt one night and I ran east on Fifth Street and cut through some houses to Fourth Street. The cop was there before I got there. I quickly turned around to run back to Fifth and when I heard the cop start to go around again, I doubled back, now he was on Fifth and I made it across Fourth and into a housing track where I lost him. When I got home, I was usually tired and sweaty and it took me awhile to sneak back in and get my adrenaline back to normal and be ready for school the next day. I always wondered if my parents knew what I was doing. They never said anything to me or challenged me, so I guess my little sister was keeping them busy. I thought I was getting away with it. Sometimes, I wished my parents or the probation Officer had caught me sneaking in and out. This was becoming a game I was beginning to like. A new behavior I would regret.

I didn't like who I was or who I was becoming and I didn't like people trying to tell me how I should act or how I should dress. Most of us wore khakis, *Frisco's*, or bell bottom pants. I tried wearing the bell bottom pants one day at school and the girls all of a sudden started talking to me, whistling and carrying on, asking who my girlfriend was or if I had one. I didn't, but there was this one girl I had a crush on. I won't mention her name 'cause she's married now and a grandmother. Besides, I didn't have the guts to ask her out and I was very shy. I did go steady with her for about a week, then got scared and broke it off because I didn't know how to handle it. When I look at it, I was hard on myself and I wasn't the conversationalist. I always seemed to stay in the background and observe the world going by me. My self-esteem was below sea level and I was beginning to like it there, where I could wallow in self-pity and whine at myself. It was my hidden world and had I known how lonely I was making it for myself, I would have tried to change it. It almost seemed like I was welcoming it, like I wouldn't feel right unless I was miserable. This was the slow sickness eating at my very soul and keeping me in a world of darkness.

The times were changing and what little I did know about the world was passing me by. I know the world scared me, especially when it got to politics. I could never figure it out. I know one time when my dad was doing things that really were scaring me. He started buying a lot of extra food and hiding it in a closet near the center of the house.

"If anything should happen, take your sister, go to the closet, cover up and hide. Stay away from the windows" he would blurt out.

It was the time of the "Cuban Missile Crisis". I remember President Kennedy talking to the nation on television. I couldn't tell what it was all about, but I knew it was serious and I trusted in my dad to do the right thing and we always did what he said. I always did like the way the President talked; he had a way of explaining things, just a little bit better to where I could almost understand. This was going on just at the time we were all headed for Junior High.

*   *   *

The September mornings of 1963 were always cold and brisk. Jackets were needed as we walked along Raitt Street. Past the new apartment complex between Monte Vista and McFadden, they extended Townsend Street. This was recently a beautiful row of eucalyptus trees and a large orange grove we could no longer play in. Joe and I would wait for Ray there and further up, we would pick-up Tommy near McFadden and continue down Raitt to Edinger. The school was called Smedley Junior High, but since the dairy was right across the street, we called it Smelly. We always stuck together and so long as we did, no one would mess with us and we weren't looking for trouble. We heard stories from our older brothers and sisters about the fights after school and the girls putting razor blades in their hair before a fight. I guess that would discourage getting jumped and anyone grabbing hair, but it sounded like a desperate measure to me. I never saw any fights like those happen.

One vivid memory of the first day of junior high was the PE class and Mr. Pomroy was the teacher. It was our first period class and still early and cold. The entire class was waiting out front of the gymnasium, joking around, goofing off and talking about where you're from and what we did for the summer. There was this one really big guy, so big he towered over us and stuck out in the crowd. He was loud, telling jokes, acting like a big shot and like he knew everything. He must have stood a foot taller than everyone else and was, as big around. He had most everyone's attention and I was talking to this one guy from New York. The New York guy said something peculiar to me. He asked me if I ever smoked *refer*. I wasn't sure what *refer* was, but I had an idea it was marijuana. I told him, "no, I never had", and he gave me a look, like I was some kind of dumb kid. I thought, "I better stay away from this guy". In the mean time, the big guy was still telling jokes and laughing with the others when the coach came. It all of a sudden got quiet and the coach had us all line up on the basketball court to take attendance.

"Alright", he said, "When I call your name, please answer with, Here!"

He started with the 'A's and continued down the alphabet. When he got to the 'G's, he said, "Sydney G". There was no answer. I was looking around to see if I could spot who Sydney "G" was and about the same time, I saw the big guy kind of looking like he was shrinking back with his head down. I said to myself, "Naw, could it be?" "Sydney "G!" the coach yelled louder. Then it happened, the big guy said, in a meek, kind of squeaky voice, "here". Just then, everyone started cracking up, stomach grabbing belly laughs, and you could hear different guys saying, "Sydney! That's his name?" all the time still laughing until the coach yelled, "O.K. that's enough!" but even he had a smirk on his face. "Answer loud and clear!" the coach barked, trying to recover a sense of civility.

The rest of the day went well meeting new people and finding out where our classes were. While I was in school, everything was fine. It was when I got out that things started to get rocky. I started hanging out with people who liked to sniff glue on the way home from school trying not to get caught. It made me paranoid and I thought everyone was out to get me. One weekend, at Ernie's house who lived on Bristol Street, along with Darrel from *Santa Nita*, we went to the Rexall drug store next to the A & P. I thought we were going to get candy until I saw Darrel pocketing a handful of Testor's model glue. My heart started to pound and I was scared of getting caught, but we made it out and went back to Ernie's house down the alley and to his garage where we hid inside and got stoned. My head was buzzing in a dream like state and at the time even saw colors in various designs. I was snapped out of it by yelling and Ernie pulling on my arm telling me to get out, my mom's coming. Ernie and I made it out, but Darrel didn't care, he stayed in the garage and we jumped the fence next door and hid by the entrance to the alley. Next thing we knew, the cops came from the other end of the alley and pulled Darrel out of the garage. Ernie and I peeked around the corner and saw the cop had Darrel by the arm taking him away. As he was being hauled away, Darrel with his other arm was emptying the tubes of glue from his pocket and dropping them in the alley. Ernie and I both had the same probation officer and getting caught together meant going back to juvenile hall. Back at school for morning nutrition, cinnamon rolls were a dime and we had a game of pitching coins at the back of the school. If you had a good day winning, you could eat all the cinnamon rolls you wanted. I kept a low profile and was comfortable being that way, but every now and then things would happen.

Another grim memory was in the auditorium watching one of those "Walter Chronkite", "You Are There" history films, when my history teacher came out, stopped the film, and announced, "the President had been shot". There was a moment of silence and then there was commotion and crying going on. I couldn't cry, but felt I should have. Some people around me were crying and some very loud. There was this black girl sitting next to me that cried out in pain and tears like she had this personal relationship with the President and it wasn't until later that I realized what that relationship was. I saw how important the President was from all the news coverage of the funeral and it was spectacular. For days afterward, they kept showing the funeral and the news constantly covered his killer repeatedly, and then his killer's, killer repeatedly. At this time, my neighborhood was predominantly black and I was more empathetic for them than I was for myself. Hispanic-Americans had not yet become nationally visible or celebrated any national origins, but it was coming. We were, so to speak, still in the *barrios* and held down, or was it people like myself holding us down?

        *   *   *

When 1964 came around, so did the Beatles and people were crazy about the Beatles. I really have to admit that the Beatles gave the world some most inspiring songs. I was having a kind of identity crisis at this time. I really didn't want to dress like a cholo anymore, and my white friends didn't like my Mexican friends. My black friends didn't like my Mexican or white friends and my Mexican friends didn't like my black friends and at the time, I didn't know how to be a diplomat. What happened? I ended up being a Mexican dressed like a surfer who didn't surf. Later I found out it didn't matter how I dressed because to the whites, I was still a Mexican and to the Mexicans I was a traitor, and to the blacks, I was some daring fool. I even got into a fight with another Mexican that was trying to be like me. I got a few swats from the vice principle and everybody got a show of two Mexicans fighting. You should have seen the other guy. He picked the fight and I finished it, although I still don't know why? It was a time when the schools had corporal punishment. It sure straightened me out, for awhile.

The following year more changes and pressure was on for all of the students. Racial tensions flowed after some altercations I didn't have anything to do with started. All the white kids were at war with anyone of another color. I tried to avoid it, but it came to me as I took a different route home. A minimum of ten whites chased me across the football field and I knew I was outnumbered so I chose flight. I jumped the fence and crossed Edinger Avenue against a red light. A black lady from my neighborhood saw what was about to happen and she pulled over and hollered at me, "get in the car". It didn't take much coaxing and I was in and off we were. The guy closest to the car threw a piece of pipe, but to no effect. Later, I found out that it started from a boyfriend-girlfriend thing turned sour. It seemed we were not ready for inter racial relationships. Thank God for that lady, because in the confusion, I never knew who she was. I knew she was from my neighborhood, but not where. Thanks lady wherever you are.

After school was out my parents sent me to my uncle's house for the summer. He lived where what is now the "South Coast Plaza" and had a lucrative construction business. My two cousins kept me busy where I learned to be a "pilot". That was working in the horse stables and I would "pile it" here and "pile it" there. I learned to train horses for the shows on the County Fair circuit and we did go from County to County. We did receive some first place ribbons and it was worth it after all the hard work it takes just to get there. I even got my picture taken in the San Diego newspaper for an article on the winners. Of course, I was not the driver, but they were glad to have a stable hand show off the winning pony.

It was summer of 1965 and when we returned home in between shows my uncle told us kids to remove the statue from the front yard. Now, this is one of those homes with a horse shoe driveway and there was a statue of a black jockey out front pointing the way ahead. We took it down, then we saw why. The Watts riots were in full swing on the television set and my uncle didn't want to offend anyone. Funny, it seemed like it was too late for that. Violence had started letting the world know that a great injustice had been brewing and people were not going to stand for it anymore. It was the first time I was to experience chaos, but kept silent, because I didn't understand it.

Silent, I seemed like I was always silent. A shadow always in the background, afraid of coming out of the shell I was in. Uninvolved with the world around me. Then snap! Suddenly someone was talking to me, and I had trouble responding unless I was doing a task or a favor for someone. Then I would move and did what I was told, because that was the only way I could operate. Later, it would become more obvious and I would be an object of use, the follower of followers.

In September of 1966, I started High School at Santa Ana Valley. My cousins were going to Mater Dei, which is a private Catholic School in Santa Ana of high regard. I was a goofy looking kid, so I thought, and a sophomore. In those days, I had a very curly head of hair that was impossible to comb to the side and it stuck up on one side, like a wedge stuck to the side of my head. It was serious curly and I had to wear a *beanie* before school just to hold it down. The dress code was strict, shirts must be tucked in and I had one of those checkered madre shirts that turn color after every wash and a matching belt, corduroys, white socks and vans tennis shoes. In those days, only poor people wore Vans, like a K-Mart stigma. No gum chewing, if caught, you would get detention. I wanted to make the best of it and always be on time to class, so I carried a briefcase bag for books, so I wouldn't have to go to my locker between classes. Being on time is one of the habits my father taught me early in life and it stuck with me. I really didn't care how I looked, and I did get a few remarks from time to time. I just had to give a certain look, like "don't even think about it" look, and I would be on my way. Partly because of my size and partly because of one of my friends, David, whom I think was the original Tasmanian Devil.

One day in History class, the teacher wrote on the board the words "Lysergic Acid Dythelimide".

"Does anyone know what this means?" When no one raised his or her hand, I raised my hand.

"I know what it is! It's LSD," I said excitingly because I knew the answer.

Then he went on to explain, what it was. Not knowing, I had singled myself out to an even lower profile and nobody would even talk to me anymore. It was like being cast out, really out. Just because I keep my ears open! On the other hand, was it because I even knew about the drugs? Drugs in those days carried a stigma. If you even smoked marijuana you were considered like a demon. Something bad that was contagious or taboo. As a sophomore, I never smoked pot and in a way I had the same sort of mentality, but not to the point of social persecution. I couldn't believe how naïve I was now that I look back. If you were from my neighborhood you just learned these things, it was all around. It surely wasn't the fact that I was a Mexican trying to fit in a white world could it be? I also didn't know that the world was about to be opened up to a new Ethnic consciousness and Civil Rights were about to explode. I don't claim to know all that happened, but one could feel the racial issue being turned around by a new generation of peace, love, drugs, waterbeds and roach clips. I got through my sophomore year unscathed, but was still trying to find my spot to fit in. I was especially attracted to the music of rock and roll. Loud and vibrating through my body in a language I could understand. I went out and tried to get into clubs at night and spend the whole night on speed or "whites" what they were called at the time. I really didn't like them cause all they did was give you gas, a dry mouth and a need to smoke one cigarette after another. I was headed down a road of trouble and pain and couldn't see my hand in front of my face.

My junior year of high school in 1967 was a little more evolutionary and positive. I did really well in school and was a typical teenager, quiet and introverted. I met a group of people from the Saunder's house in the south part of Santa Ana. Mrs. Saunder was a single mom with three boys, all teens Troy, Steve, and Ted Saunder of whom I would consider peers. She understood what it was like to be a teenager. She cared about us as kids and knew we needed a place to gather. A place that was safe from drugs or any negative influence teenager's fall into and we could socialize. I didn't know what a peer was until I met the boys. We became friends and learned to socialize expressing each other feelings, ideas, and dreams. Troy knew all about rock n' roll music and he remembered most all songs, their artists, when released and how much each album cost. I admired Troy very much for his intellect on music. Most of all, I could relate to it without feeling uncomfortable. Many teenage girls would came over. It was a different experience speaking to girls at the same level. They treated me like a friend rather than an adversary or someone who was just interested in sex. They also made me feel comfortable. It was also a place to find out about parties and we liked parties. Every day was a new experience and fun. We met daily and it was a place to gather with twenty to twenty-five kids everyday. We just hung out, went to dances on the weekends to the Rondeveaux in Balboa the Cinnamon Cinder in Long Beach.

At first, it seemed harmless because although the Saunder group felt everything was all right, there still was another factor. A small few of the group was out smoking pot. They would miss a few days, then come back. Miss a few more days, until days became weeks, then come back. I was unaware of the two factors and too ignorant of what was going on. I knew something bad was going on, but I guess I was too afraid to admit it to myself or to the others. It was something we didn't discuss. I knew the ones who parted ways were too ashamed to return and eventually never returned. From the remarks that went around, I didn't want anything to do with it. It became apparent after a time. I didn't know that I would become one of them.

We had most of our fun during the summer playing baseball, then football with other groups from different areas of town. We met all sorts of people just like us. It was the first time I met a group of all Mexicans called, "The Street Masters". A car club from my old Artesia Barrio. I like the thought of a car club. Now that was positive and at a time when people needed to be brought together. "Why can't we do something like that?" I thought.

Soon, we all joined a club. Now this wasn't a gang, I didn't like the gang scene and knew as a Mexican, I would be an open target for the police. This group was a mixture of Mexicans, Samoans, Whites, Dutch Indonesians, Blacks, Germans, Italians, Filipinos, French Canadians and Peruvians. Most all of us were second or third generation immigrants. Some longer, but we all had something in common. We were teens looking to make sense of a world of cultural change and chaos. We were called, "The Griffins" and had jackets with an insignia of a lion with talons on the back. We played Football with the car clubs, went to the beach often, cruised the boulevards from Santa Ana, Newport Beach, Whittier, Hollywood, and had parties and we were generally a well-mannered group of guys and girls with no trouble in mind. We often met at the Jack-In-The-Box on Bristol to eat, but if anyone else saw us there, they'd think we're on their turf. I didn't even know what turf was.

There was other car clubs, like "The Classics", "Sigma Phi", and "The Chevy Nova's". All car clubs looking to get a better edge on the other clubs. Most of the others were either Mexican or White, but we were the only ones who could express all culture clubs. It was a positive step for teens to stay away from gangs and take pride in building cars with an attitude. It was either a low rider or a souped up muscle car. We also had car races down the coast highway between Newport and Huntington Beach. I once raced a 327 Chevy Nova against a 327 Chevy El Camino and won by a very short distance. It was an exhilarating experience and thankful to my friend Art for letting me use his El Camino. Art and I were *"Road Dogs"* at the time and went everywhere together.

In 1968, times were changing and I was finally caught for ditching school and was sent to Mountain View continuation in Santa Ana. I heard stories about this school and that it was cool. Somehow, it seemed just like I sabotaged my life just to get there. On one hand, I was shamed at not completing and graduating from Valley High and on the other I had crossed the line of being with the in-crowd or all the misfits and troubled students. I still never admitted my troubles and it was my way of rebelling, but didn't know what I was rebelling against. At Mountain View, you were given a set of books and instructed to have them completed by the end of the year. If you feel tired you could go to sleep at your desk and no one would bother you. I got tired of that and finished all my books way before the end of the year. The thing that I most remember was the fact that working at your own pace gives you a drive to do work with interest and excitement I hadn't felt in a long time. I was out of school at twelve p.m. and I had a job at a hardware store in Santa Ana called "Consumer City". In those days, I could work from one to nine p.m. and save money to buy a car.

Although I kept busy I still was a bit confused and trying pot made it worse and made me paranoid. When I first tried the pot, I did on my own an experiment. I obtained a joint and smoked it while driving alone. Big mistake, I didn't know that I suddenly was doing 15-MPH in a 40-MPH zone. On top of that, it took me over an hour to get to where I was going only fifteen minutes away. I kept stopping at stop signs that were 100 feet ahead. I was zoned, and paranoid.

I did graduate at the top of my class and got a whole fifty-dollar scholarship to a community college. When I did get to college, I could not relate to the courses or the students and felt stupid. It wasn't working for me and I liked school, but I still dropped out.

There was a time when I had first started regularly smoking pot towards the end of 1969. I was with a group of guys from the Saunder's house near McFadden Junior High School. Mrs. Saunder didn't know that any of us had indulged in smoking pot or taking LSD. We were all friends and each didn't want the others to know that they were smoking pot. The groups started to break up into different factions, each not wanting the other to know about the pot smoking. There were other factors, like who put money into buying the pot in the first place and who to share it with.

My father had just bought me a used car, a 1958 Mercedes Benz with four doors, a hydromatic transmission and the interior still had a fresh smell of leather. It was old but nice and excellent to cruise around in especially down by the beach.

We were in two groups; each equipped with a joint or two. Italian Dave and I drove the one block to the school. I wasn't sure where to park so I parked the car next to a house that was being built across the street from the school and I could see it from there. Dave and I were out behind the school *toking* on a *joint*. Bennie, Jim and Steve went out to play a trick on me. While I was gone, they pushed my car into the garage that was being built. Not noticing, the neighbor watching them and calling the police for suspicious persons. They left, laughing and carrying on acting stupid and silly while Dave and I finished the joint we had consumed and snorted the last up our nose.

Walking back to the car, I noticed the police inspecting my car and stopped. Looking at the scene, my heart started pounding with paranoia setting in. I thought someone called the police on us and we were smoking dope, eyes red as the early moon. I jolted to run and the sudden movement caught the attention of the police officer. He yelled something, but Dave and I both ran into the brush behind the school. We ran hard and I had the worse case of *cottonmouth* I ever experienced and all I could say was "Oh Shit I dun it now". Dave suggested we go around the park and through the tract of homes and back to the car. While walking and watching the police my thoughts were lost in paranoia and quickly going down into a stupor of self inflicting emotional battery, cussing at times, muttering to myself. Dave probably thought I was going crazy after all, and I said out loud, "I was just being chased by the police for stealing my own car! Is that stupid or what". At that, Dave started laughing at the irony of that and I guess it was funny. When we got back to the Saunders and told the story, you could see they were holding back from laughing and being serious, but when I told them I was being chased for stealing my own car they all got a good laugh. Somehow, it just didn't seem as funny to me.

Vietnam was a big subject and some people I new joined the service to go. Nothing in the news or papers ever discussed in detail what was really going on over there. I also didn't fully understand when Martin Luther King Jr. was assassinated and when Robert Kennedy was killed. I thought these were the good guys and who would want to kill them. I didn't know that the turmoil I was feeling was being felt by the whole United States.

All the music industry made music of peace and love, but the world seemed to be killing each other left and right. It was around this time that I started playing drums in a blues band. We weren't really a band, but a bunch of guys learning a new style of expression. We played in the garage at my father's house on Westeria. It attracted a lot of attention but we kept the hours and music down to a small roar. For awhile playing the blues seemed like a form of expression I could relate too. We kept pot smokin and it seemed that was as far as any of us would go.

Some started going on to other drugs, like *LSD* and reds, which were downers (*seconal*) that would give you a don't give a f__k attitude and wreck a lot of cars and lives. The *LSD* became an almost daily event and I got to a point where I wouldn't take *LSD* unless I had a pocket full of reds to come down with. I was enjoying the escape and it was a good hiding place from myself. Being in a band attracted lots of drugs and people always gave it to you. High technology for us was to go to Hollywood for the opening premier of "2001 A Space Odyssey" and get way out in front and lay before the screen just to see the last part when the rush of colors come at you and your frying on *LSD.*

We heard about the MyLai Massacre, but nobody knew what it was really all about. We did know that it was a slaughter of a small village of three hundred. The government had kept it secret so information was scarce until later in the year. We knew it was an atrocity created by a frustrated platoon. In addition, that to speak of the conduct of American soldiers was forbidden.

This is when two of my peers Joe (Junie) and Troy got drafted and sent to Vietnam. The draft was a lottery back then and I had a very low lottery number meaning I was not going and I wasn't about to volunteer. My other peer, Ben Libay had the same birthday as I did, so we knew, at least we wouldn't go. Other peers got drafted, like Ron, Phil, Troy, and my cousin John Salgado. Little did we know about the horrors over there until they wrote back and little did we know of the ones who didn't make it back home.

We continued to use drugs, mostly smoking pot and hallucinogens. My hair grew with the times and by this time I had big Afro style hair and was considered a hippie. I attended concerts such as Led Zeppelin, Fleetwood Mac, Almond Brothers and our band was playing more into the Desrali Gears, and Black Sabbath. We tried our own album and got aired once on a local radio station, but the drugs took a toll on the members and the band slowly fell apart.

Early in the year1970, I was working for a printed circuit company and proud of the name, "National Technology". It sounded like I worked for an All-American secret technology or worked for the government when people saw my check or something of the sort. Little did I know then, how it was going to affect my ideals and my way of thinking. I still swear to this day that this company was pouring dangerous chemicals right into the local sewer system.

I was making printed circuit boards for computers, missiles and automated equipment. I was good at what I did and worked about 60 hours a week and continued to take drugs to stay up and drugs to slow down. I met lots of new friends; some are what I call the Japanese connection. It was with these people that I got involved in running drugs to Hawaii and thinking I was taking a vacation, I was actually used as a mule. I only went for two weeks, but ended up staying on the island for three months. With my hair the way it was, I fit right in. I looked like a local and after picking up on the *pigeon talk*, I was a local.

When I had the chance, I went snorkeling, just with a snorkel, mask, fins and a spear off the reef at Makaha. I would dive and go to depths beyond my capability, but it was so beautiful I had to continue. There was a time when I was so astounded by the beauty of the sea that it brought to me a peace of mind, like a freedom I had not experienced ever. I jumped down in the reefs, lost in its beauty, surrounded by silence from the outside world except for my breathing and the rhythm of my heart. I was mesmerized by the surroundings and continued to explore the awesome feeling of peace and contentment when I came upon an eel. It was a moray eel, looking out of the rocks, with it's big head gasping for air, taking in big gulps of water, like it was breathing it in it's natural state and I was out of my element. I was stunned, and contemplating shooting it with a spear, wondering what it would taste like.

I remembered a warning that my brother told me, "If you come up on an eel, and you decide to shoot it, you better not miss, because if it bites you, it will not let go until it takes a big chunk out of you". I looked at the eel and had my spear right on his head, but the vision my brother had implanted took precedence and I moved on, giving a peace sign.

Not noticing the time that had expired, I looked up and the surface of the water and it was a long way away above me with the sun shining down through the ripples of water, glimmering, teasing me, testing me to see if I could make it to the top. I suddenly realized that I was overdue on air and headed for the surface, fins kicking like hell to get there. When I broke the surface, I gasped for air like no one had ever gasped before. I almost drowned and didn't know it. Nature played a trick on me that day, but nature was never so beautiful as that moment. Nature is funny too, because also one day at Makaha, I was walking ankle deep on the reef and found a place to jump off the reef into the deep blue sea. I jumped in holding my mask and through the bubbles, I was face to face with a large parrotfish. I swear, I was just as startled as he was and the expression of surprise, shock, disbelief all at once hit us both and we both turned to swim away in opposite directions just as fast as we could.

I remember one particular evening sitting on the reef rocks at Makaha beach, watching the sunset and thinking about what I was going to do with my life. I kept the scene of the orange and rose cutting through the distant clouds in my head to remember for all time. I was lost, and the loneliest person in the happiest place on earth. I didn't know who I was, in constant fear of life I suppose. I just couldn't get it. What it was all about? People kept using me, or should I say, I let them use me. My relationships with women were scary. I love women, but I was not comfortable with the word, "love", unless it was meant in the sense of brotherly love from the Flower Movement. Hippies I thought, everyone really loved each other, but all I saw was a form of use in one way or another. People wanting to be your friend because you had something they wanted. You didn't know or were too innocent to know what that was. It was time to go back to the mainland. I sold my Volkswagen van to have enough money to send my little brother back that was visiting also.

When I returned to the mainland and started a new life, I got word that my peer Junie had died in Vietnam. It was the first time I cried in many years and I wanted to know why? The stories that spread was different and it frightened me to the bone. Junie was an avid follower of Jimi Hendricks, who just recently died of an overdose. It was said, that Jimi just wanted to cross the threshold of death and look inside. Like looking through another door and peek at the other side. He didn't make it back and I feared Junie did the same. Junie received an honorable burial and I helped carry his casket. His mother wanted it that way. I felt so guilty, because although we wrote often, Junie had left me to care for his girlfriend of which, I did an awful job. I did take her out to dinner, to the show and kept her company.

Junie found another love in Vietnam, a girl by the name of Chen-Che. He wanted me to tell his girlfriend here, but I couldn't do it. How could I tell her he's in love with another woman? I felt obligated, but still couldn't. I buried it, because I loved her too and didn't know how to express it and deal with my own inadequacies. I felt that if I fell in love with her, that I would be crossing a trusted friendship. I was also angry with Junie, because I thought his new girlfriend was using him to get into this country. They found him dead in his bunk and I always thought that she had given him an overdose, just to get one more GI soldier. I never did find out which story it was and it was too painful to think about.

1971 brought a year of frustration and loneliness. I was 21 and supposed to be a grown man, but I spent most of the time smoking pot, going to parties, taking *ludes, rainbows, mescaline, acid* and anything that was cool. I also met a lot of people who were heavy into the drug scene. I went to parties where there might've been a full ounce of heroin or cocaine on a coffee table for anyone to use and enjoy. I attended parties in fancy homes in Laguna Beach where the rich blended in with the little people. *Waterpipes* were everywhere just to see who had the best, biggest, coolest *waterpipe*. Seeing who could take the biggest drag without coughing it up? We were all heading into a world of self-destruction in the name of peace and love.

By the end of 1972, I rode a bicycle to work after a few set backs and saved enough money to buy a car. It was a "Toyota Celica" and was 1 year old, but that was as new as I ever got. It was also the time that some of the ones who stayed here and didn't get drafted got introduced to the mother of all drugs, heroin.

Of our peer group, Wolf was the first to start. We saw the change in him, admired part of it and detested the rest swearing we would never do that. At the time Wolf, Bennie, his wife Chris, and I all lived in the same three-bedroom home we rented in south Santa Ana. We all worked at "National" except for Chris. I also had a dog that I adopted from an owner who tried to kill him with an overdose of *seconal*. Sam was his name and Sam was a big, black, "Great Dane". Sam turned out to be not as stupid as his previous owner thought he was. Sam and I went everywhere together and I swear he could read my thoughts and knew ahead of time what I was going to do. It's hard to explain, but we had this connection and without training. He knew my command and knew what I wanted.

Bennie borrowed my car one evening and took my dog Sam with him. He had taken a few *reds* and frankly, so did I, so I could have cared less if he got hurt or not. *Reds* do that to you. About an hour later, Sam came scratching at the door. When I opened it, Sam ran in and looked scared and he continued looking back outside and back to me. I asked him, "where's Bennie!" And he looked back outside with fear in his eyes and I knew Bennie was hurt or got into a wreck. Sure enough, after a few phone calls Chris made and me backtrailing the roads, Bennie was all right and he did wreck. He spiraled my car to a twisted wreck of metal. All sides were bent and scratched up and it was the first time the car was wrecked. Sam was all right too. Drugs were taking our lives little by little and the trap was set.

"Going Down"
(Into the pit)

◆

One evening in 1972 after a long day at work, I came home and put some Jeff Beck on the stereo. A song called "Going Down." Wolf was fixing a syringe full of heroin ready to shoot the dark liquid into the pit of his arm. Then he turned and asked, "want some?" It was the perfect moment and my first try at the lady dragon, heroin. It was another experiment to try and find out why Junie had died for this drug. It's ironic because that's exactly what was going to happen to me. I was "going down" to the pits of hell and I couldn't see it coming because this drug was like it was from God. I was too scared to put the needle in my arm, so Wolf did it for me. I was naïve of the ritual of preparing the dope, cooking it in a spoon, and filing the syringe that would haunt me after the first time.

My "first rush", would lead me into an endless trek to attain it, just one more time. I was in a state of ecstasy, suddenly released from the pain of hiding my feelings. I was released from the fears that haunted my being for so many years, like a flood pouring out of me. I could feel peace, true happiness and a sense of one, being with the universe. It was like taking a combination of all the drugs I have taken and finally finding the right one. With the feeling of coming out of a stupor and sweat pouring out of me, I yelled, "Yes! Yes! This is so f__king awesome. God damn me! God

F_king! Damn Me!" With that, I felt an urge coming up from the pit of my stomach and threw up the hot, acidic bile I had in there.

After the initial induction into a new realm, I sat in my easy chair, turned up the sounds and went into a dream world where I could be half into the surreal and half in the real. It's like you could be dreaming and although your eyes are closed, you still have a very definite sense of what's going on around you. Like being in two places at the same time, or occupying two points of the same space at the same time. I suddenly forgot all the times I told myself, I would never, never, do that drug. I forgot all the times I talked with people, my peers, about how we despised junkies and it made them steal, rob, and do bad things, anything to get the drug, like crossing over to a new life of "criminal behavior". "That will never happen to me," I thought. After all, I had plenty of drugs. I didn't know I was about to enter a world of denial and excuses. What did I have to worry about?

I continued to use. Sparingly at first, snorting at parties, and I began to lose weight. I began to feel what it was like "not" to have the drug in my system. Sick! Very sick! But it was too late; the lady dragon had me by the balls. As time past, Wolf got busted for selling a gram of heroin to an undercover cop. After a lengthy court scene, he got a year in the county jail and I took his girlfriend to visit him on a regular basis. The facility was in the South part of the county and was minimum security. Wolf had a beautiful girl friend, and the thought never entered my mind about others seeing her as the same. We had what I call a more loving and intellectual relationship. We were true friends. When I saw the other inmates look at her with wanting eyes, I felt a bit disturbed and protected her the way Wolf would have wanted, but in a different way. Wolf and I were like brothers. He knew I would treat his girlfriend also like a brother would treat a sister. I knew he would understand and he did.

When we finally got together in a visiting booth, I was beginning to see the error of my ways. Wolf looked clean and healthy from working the weights and seemed to be tougher in attitude. That's when I started a path for cleaning up.

Around 1973, I got my car back from the accident Bennie had. Bennie felt bad about the crash and I felt bad because he felt bad. My self-esteem was so low I felt that there was nothing I could do that was right. Everything I did turned out wrong as if negativity followed me around.

I was still in denial but didn't know it at the time. I thought I could kick an existing heroin habit on my own. Actually, It was a time where I believed in myself for short periods and tried real hard. It was a time of constantly having a sick feeling and pretending nothing was wrong.

One of the girls at work of whom I had a crush on invited me to a softball game at a local park. I thought it would be an excellent opportunity to get out and take Sam along to the park. Sam always attracted attention anywhere we went. I walked Sam around the park and I watched the game from a distance, all the time telling myself I was going to be all right and my life was going to be back on the right track again. I had high hopes and was even a little proud of the short distance I was building between the drug and me.

The game was over and I made small talk with the girls and we parted ways. I had a crush on her and we worked together for many years. I found it very difficult to talk to her and things came out all wrong. I put my foot in my mouth every step of the way. I decided I'd had enough. My conversation was weak and I felt trapped. We parted ways.

It was on my way home, that I made another mistake. I passed a nightclub near Harbor and Garden Grove Blvd in the city of Garden Grove. I was feeling edgy and a little nervous, so I went in to take the edge off. I left Sam in the car and cracked the windows for him. He had a habit of slobbering all over the windows anyway and the weather was cool outside, so he was safe. I had heard of this club and wanted a look inside to see the atmosphere. Me with my big head of hair looking like a crossbreed of a Black Mexican hippie in a Saturday Night Fever environment. I walked across and through the tables and could see girls and the DJ on stage practicing dance moves to the music for the evening crowd.

I sat at a table where I could observe and have a drink. I ordered a tequila gimlet and thanked the waitress. When she returned with my drink, I looked at it for a moment, thought about it being a drug too, and took a small sip. I set my glass down and in the same moment on my right side, I felt a powerful blow to the backside of my rib cage. Before I could even figure out what that was, I got another from the left side and then I was up in the air. I felt arms all around me. My head hit a door and I was in the air, where my head hit a cement column on the outside sidewalk. I was unconscious for a moment. I looked up and Sam was trying to get out of the car, scratching at the door and window, trying desperately to get out. I turned around and four Marine-looking guys were closing the door where we had just come out. They were laughing. I was pissed and went to the car and let Sam out. He was pissed and we headed for the door. They locked it from the inside and I banged on it yelling for them to come out. I kept yelling, "one on one", "come on, one on one." I walked to another entrance, but it was locked too.

I sat on the edge of the curb rubbing my head when a Police Cruiser pulled up and asked me what was going on. I told the officer, "that's what I would like to know?" He told me to put my hands behind my back, searched me for weapons and handcuffed me. Sam was puzzled and so was I. But now he had a worried look because of the handcuffs. I explained that I had ordered a drink and was jumped from behind. The officer stayed by the door and was talking to the management. From his gestures, I could see he was making it out to be my entire fault. I told Sam, "Hey bud, it doesn't look too good, but don't worry I'll get you home".

About that time, a guy came out from the inside and started talking to the officer. I never knew who he was but after a few minutes the officer came over to me and told me he was from Huntington Beach and saw me come into the club. He confirmed what I told the officer. I remember the officer asked me if I was all right as he took the handcuffs off. I told him I thought I was O.K. but I had a headache. He said he could call an ambulance, but I said I didn't think I needed one. That was my second mistake, not wanting to bother anyone as usual. The officer excused me and told me to go home and that I took a pretty good blow to the head.

I got Sam back into the car. We were both nervous and were settling down a bit from all the excitement. I left the parking lot to the on-ramp of the 5 Freeway southbound and that was all I remember.

When I woke, I was facing the traffic in the opposite direction against the center divider and on the fence. A Highway Patrol Officer was banging on my window for me to wake up and open the door. I hit my head again in the accident and I was handcuffed again and told I was under arrest for drunk driving. They also arrested Sam and for sure, I know he didn't do anything and didn't deserve to go to the pound. This is the second time the car was wrecked.

I was taken to U.C.I. Medical Center for a blood test and then taken to the Orange County Jail for processing. I tried to explain what happened and for the Highway Patrol Officer to check with the Garden Grove Police Department, but they acted as if this happened all the time and was a regular occurrence. I was waiting in the holding cell with a migraine headache by this time. I was starting to feel sorry for myself and let my guard down. I sat on the floor and tried to fall asleep, worried about Sam, crashing my car for the second time and in despair because everything turned to mud.

I woke with a loud noise and scuffling. I looked out of the cell and saw a Sheriff Deputy on top of an inmate, pinned down by his knees. He was trying to cut the inmate in the face with a ring, a very big ring. The inmate did his best, trying to move his head so as not to get hit. Other Deputies were just standing around watching this go down. I yelled out and said, "leave him alone!"

The Deputy hitting the inmate said to me, "shut up! Your next!"

Sure enough, when they got the other inmate into a cell, they came in after me. I was next, and when they got me out of the cell, they tried to break my back. His knee was in my back and he was choking me with his forearm while the other Deputies held my legs and arms. Whatever he asked me I couldn't answer back, so they choked until I almost passed out. When they did let up, they grabbed me from all four limbs and literally threw me into a small holding cell where I hit the back of the cell with my head and passed out.

I don't know how long I lay in there, but I heard a rattling of keys and when the door opened, they said, "Morales, you're being released!" I tried to get up, but I had a hard time standing and a hard time walking. I walked as if I was drunk, but I wasn't. I had a concussion and didn't know it.

When I got to the outside gate, my two friends Susan and Linda were there outside waiting for me. They helped me to their car and took me to the Santa Ana Hospital. All the time I was in a dreamlike state wondering, is this just punishment, Lord? All I wanted to do was get out, go to the park, kick a habit. "It can't get any worse than this!" I said to myself. I was feeling sorry for myself again.

In the hospital I was rushed in and checked over my whole body. I had bruises all over; my ribs felt like they were kicked in and my back ached with pain. My legs were made of rubber and my head was a daze with blurred vision and my ears were ringing. The hospital staff put me on an EEG machine. They later said I had a slight concussion. I thought, "slight concussion! I feel like I was run over by a truck". I was tired, very tired and went to sleep.

The night brought nightmares and visions of the dead, all my life seemed hopeless and I was stuck in a bottomless pit. All my energies seemed for nothing and what little faith in God that I had left was about to be brought out into the light. The following day I decided to just say, "f__k it! This life is a bunch of bullshit and I want to fix".

I called my connection Jesse and instructed him to bring me some dope, now! I was mad at the world and why shouldn't I be. I fell back into a sleep and when I woke there was a Santa Ana Police Officer standing over my bed with a nurse. He had a bible in his hand and I knew I had my wits about me, because at the same instant I knew Jesse had put the dope in the bible. The Officer asked if this was my bible, "Ah Christ!" I said to myself. He was trying to trap me. One more time, I had to deny God. I told him "no, that's not my bible." Now I really did feel like dirt, one, because I was scared of getting caught and another, because I wanted the drug more than God. I just bought myself some time, so I could get just one more fix. That's just the way it happened and I'll always remember the religious significance that instance had on me.

I waited for the cop to leave and checked myself out of the hospital, which took some doing because they warned me that I was responsible and it was against the doctors advise, blah, blah, blah. I took a taxi to Jesse's apartment, which was in the city of Garden Grove. On the way, my mind was making me sicker than I really was. It's that dominant thinking causing anxiety about getting the next fix.

I didn't have any cab fare. I told the cabby, I would give him the money when I collected it and bring it back down to him and left him my driver's license for collateral. What a dummy, I could have just taken off, but I came back with the money for him.

*   *   *

I continued using the drug and eventually lost my best friends, as well as losing my job, and losing my self-respect. I continued fixing, going through the ritual of finding the dope, finding a safe place to fix. While fixing, which became a ritual, because it was a good feeling to *cop* a bag of dope, unwrap your bag of goodies, which contained a q-tip, or for the lower class dopefiend, a cigarette butt filter, a large spoon which never got filled to the top. More was better, so we thought until someone cut the dope for sale a little lite, and people died. There was also a plastic binky; a combination of a push-up popsicle stick, attached to a *chuppie* with a rubber band, all wrapped in a bandana, which was used to tie off and a pack of sulfur matches. Just add water, a little dope, a match and *Q-Vo!* You got high. To this day, when I catch the smell of sulfur matches, I get sick and feel like vomiting, just like the ritual that took place before a fix.

I got my car back again and Sam got released and I was feeling low, so low I had to give Sam away. I couldn't afford him anymore because I put the dope money before him. I couldn't support him and a drug habit. When I went out I was afraid of myself, nothing was right. I saw the signs but failed to heed. The lowered head, couldn't look people in the eye. Everything was a lie and my mind, body and spirit were in the darkness of self-destruction. It was like I didn't want to live in this body anymore, like I was trying to get out.

One late evening traveling south on Fairview Avenue just past First Street the road curved. It had trees in the middle and in an instant I hit the gas, straight for the trees. The car careened when it hit the curb and I missed the tree and flew to the other side of the road. Thank God there was no one on the road. I was still fish tailing and I hit the gas again, and again it hit the curb, missed another tree, but this time I lost control. On the other side, I crashed into and through a brick wall and was knocked unconscious. When I woke, the paramedics were removing me from the wreckage. I was only bruised! The car had its third strike and was totaled and almost went into a mobile home. The only reason I was upset was because I couldn't even do this right. I was a total failure. I cannot describe the feelings I was going through losing what seemed everything. I said to myself, "God, what do you want?" "What is it? That I can't even die! I guess it isn't my time or I must be one of the luckiest losers in the world."

I kept getting arrested for under the influence of a narcotic, burglary, driving under the influence of a narcotic. It got so stupid that one time

I was arrested for falling asleep while in line at an In-An-Out Burgers on Bristol Street. I was past out, *stoned* out of my mind. Luckily, the car was in park, so the Police gave me a room for 10 days. I got arrested so many times I lost count. I was plagued with skin disorders and my health was in a careless mode. I practiced self-mutilation and I wouldn't eat right and drank alcohol and did drugs to obliteration.

The judge finally gave me some time to think about what I was doing, so gave me 30 days, then 90 days and I was still going to court for the burglary of which I got two years in prison. Now, about this time I had a piece habit, meaning I had mostly all the drugs I wanted. There was lapses in between in which I had to steal or scam to make ends meet, but my system had a lot of drugs in it. At times, I thought I had more drugs, than blood in me. In jail, I got very ill and was put in a dorm setting, since I was a *lightweight*. I couldn't eat, and vomited constantly. At times, I would vomit out of my mouth and nose, urinate, and defecate all at the same time. I swear I had stuff coming out every orifice at once, literally.

This is where I met Chava. He was quite a colorful character and his only reason for living was to get some more dope. He brought me medicine, for my nerves; chocolate to curb my cravings, and food (candy bars), when I couldn't get my own. He had a real knack for obtaining these items and of course I wandered what he wanted in return. As it turned out, he just wanted another connection for when he got out again. He was glad to help, since help was scarce and the jailers could care less of how sick you are until it's too late. Chava was a *veterano*, from the *old school*, and he constantly talked. He told me, if your going to fix, do it right, fix in your right arm with your left hand and get used to it. When the cops pull you over, they usually look at your left arm first, because most people are right handed, so keep your left arm clean of tracks. I had to laugh at myself when that trick worked for the first time and I got away from the police several times, still not knowing, it was all just a matter of time.

He also talked about tattoo's and said, "don't ever put tattoos on, once you do, you don't want to stop and in six months, you'll wonder, what the hell was I thinking when I put this crap on?" So I never put any tattoos on, except for one. I was really sick and just copped a bag of dope. I pulled over to a curb and not having any water with me, I opened the car door and took water from the curb gutter, put it in my bottle cap spoon, cooked it with my dope, drew it up through a piece of cigarette filter into the syringe. When I put it in my arm, the needle clogged. I was sweating and my nose was running and I kept looking up and around to see if I wasn't found out. "Hurry up!" I said, and lit a match to the needle to unclog it. It worked, but I didn't even clean the soot off, I just shoved it in my arm and squeezed off the syringe. The carbon on the needle left a tattoo in the ditch of my arm. I didn't realize how I could stoop so low. Chava talked about that too, "just do what you gotta do *homes*," he would say. I had it in my mind that tattoos were the mark of the beast and never would I get one.

Self-respect was a concept I was not familiar with, but I would soon learn maybe a different version of it. Self-respect amongst inmates and society are very different sets of values. Self-respect to a dope fiend is to burn every bridge you can. Rob, steal, scam, and do whatever to get that next fix before you get caught. Chava would say, "ride till the wheels fall off." Society says, do everything you can like using that energy you use to rob, steal, scam and whatever to stay off the drugs, and turn it around. I tried it and soon after I was released, I found out I didn't have the stamina to keep that frame of mind and I was off using again and running from the probation officer.

In 1975 one evening I was hanging with a couple of people. One was a girl I previously met in the lobby of the jail as I was being released. I looked at her, she looked at me and immediately, we knew we wanted the same thing, a fix and off we went. It turned out she turned tricks for her habit and was quite street wise. The guy, all I knew was that he had a car and the girl brought him along. We had just made some money and went to the Delhi Barrio to *cop*. It wasn't much, but just enough for a bag to split three ways. I knew of this guy just from sight and the girl with us knew him. We gave him the money to *cop* for us. Now we had to split it four ways, if it gets any worse than this, you might as well forget it, but we were sick and desperate.

The guy burned us and never came back to the spot we agreed on. Damn, I was pissed for being so stupid. I told the guy with the car to drive around the *barrio*. He was a white dude with a county tattoo of a star on his forearm, so I thought, he must be all right. I spotted the guy who burned us and told the driver to pull over.

The driver and the girl looked scared and said, "what are you going to do?"

"Get the dope or the money," I replied.

When I approached the house and saw him, he looked at me like he was just caught. I didn't see the bat lying next to the fence by the entry-way where the mailbox was. At the same time, his friend came over from the side of the house. I said, "look, just give me the money or the dope." He said, he didn't have it, the money or the dope. I knew they already fixed the dope, because a long time had already lapsed and they had plenty of time. Now this guy was known as being ruthless, but I had a little streak also.

"Well, I suggest you better come up with something quick," I said.

He started walking toward me, slowly.

"Look, we can do this easy or the hard way, but we already got a bunch of Mexicans fighting Mexicans and that doesn't look good at all." I started backing off now as both of them approached me slowly. The other guy had something in his hand and I didn't know if it was a screw-driver or a knife, but I slowly backed up.

"You think this is going to prove anything?" I said as I slowly reached for my belt buckle.

I backed up and removed my belt; I passed the bat leaning against the fence. He saw it and picked it up. Suddenly realizing my situation, I wrapped my belt and buckle in my hand with the buckle end coming out from my index finger and thumb on my right hand. I barely glanced back at the car and the two were yelling at me to get in the car. The big guy took a swing at my head and I tried to catch it, but caught it on my left wrist, breaking it. That started it. I also caught the other guy in the face with the belt buckle. That backs them up for the moment and I could hear the girl in the car screaming at the driver to come help me. He didn't, the big guy told him to stay out of it or he was dead. My wrist was in pain, but a pain I had no time to feel for a more important reason, staying alive. We circled and he came with the bat again, this time the bat broke in two pieces, right on my left forearm. I got a couple of strikes in myself, when I felt a punch in my right side. It was a knife. Stunned, both of them pushed me back towards the car and I got in a couple of punches in, when I felt two more punches in my chest. They had me back against the car hood. I knew that if I didn't do anything and right now, I would be dead.

The big guy yelled at the little guy to, "get the gun, get the gun in the back."

With that, and I don't know where it came from, but I literally pushed both of them up and back off of me. My ride took off and I could see from the shadows in the rear window, the girl was beating on the guy to turn around. As I ran toward the car, they suddenly stopped and backed up and I got in on the driver side passenger door. Tires burned and we were gone!

It was over as quick as it started. I was bleeding bad and when we passed under a street light, I could see my tee shirt under my pendelton was red with blood and blood was still oozing out. They drove me to the closest hospital, which was "Coastal Hospital" on Bristol Street. Once there, the girl ran into the emergency room to tell them what happened. She came back out and said, "do you have any insurance?" I was astounded by the question.

"F__k No! I'm just bleeding to death!" I replied.

She ran back in and was back in a few seconds. I could hear her yelling obscenities at them while gesturing as she ran. They refused to treat me since I didn't have any insurance, and by law, they had a right to do so at this time. So much for broken promises to heal the sick and injured. They gladly called ahead to another hospital in the City of Orange called Chapman General where I was born.

By that time, I lost a lot of blood and the back of the car was full of blood. I was starting to pass out and feel weak and cold, like I was being drained of life, seeing a darkness surrounding the street lights as was passed under each one in a blur. "Hurry" I yelled and all this time the girl was yelling at the driver calling him a "bitch" and a "punk". Luckily, there was a team of doctors and nurses waiting for me. As soon as I got on the gurney, I passed out for a moment and during that moment, I could hear all the voices of the hospital staff fussing over me, taking off my clothes, cutting fabric, tugging here and there, probing my chest area. I tried to wake up but couldn't and I could feel my body being moved and lights would blink off and on as we passed through the hallways to the emergency room.

I woke with pain when someone probed the hole in my side with a long cotton Q-tip to see how deep the wound was. They asked if I could hear them and with a weak nod, I nodded, yes. A nurse said, "don't worry, we're going to take good care of you." Then she shouted out commands to get a catheter. When they placed the catheter, it hurt worse than the stab wound. They also had all kinds of tubes coming out of me in places I never knew I had and an oxygen mask on my face. As it turned out, the stab wound was not as bad as it felt when the knife was going in. The knife blade hit my side at a 90-degree angle to my ribs, meaning it didn't pass through. Had it been turned slightly, it would gone through the rib cage and punctured my lung. The other two stab wounds hit the bone in my breastplate and didn't go through, but it sure did bleed a lot. Luckily, it was only a pocketknife, had it been a dagger or Bowie survival knife, I would be dead.

I stayed in the intensive care unit and when I woke, I saw my mother and sister coming in the door. My sister let out this blood curling type of yell and moan combined that hit me in a spot I was unfamiliar with. In that moment, I could feel her pain and love, anger and frustration over me. It communicated to a depth I feared to travel into my very soul and stirred an emotion I'll never forget. I began to weep, not for me, but for her, my sister, who always took care of me when I was younger. She sometimes hated me for it, because I took a part of her life taking care of me. I was always in the way of her teen years. Mom always told her to take me with her or go with me when I went to play baseball or football. She never knew why my parents were all of sudden so protective of me. She practically raised me and in that moment, I finally felt the connection I had lost in a world of pain I had created for myself. I realized just how much a sisters love could extend itself and reach out to me. I felt a chill go through me and although I didn't like it, I felt good, like a homecoming of sorts. For a moment, I could feel again.

Later, my oldest brother Michael came in to visit and all I could do was laugh, telling him, "don't worry I'll get out of this one somehow". He also experienced lots of pain seeing me overdose too many times. Turning blue with no breath in me along with my little sister Monica calling the paramedics to come get me. Somehow I always got saved.

The very next day out of the hospital, with a cast on my left arm and a wrist fracture, pain in my bruised chest, I got into another fight and lost.

I was jealous over a girlfriend. The girlfriend I was left in charge of from my friend Junie. I let the air out of her new boyfriend's tires. I got busted for it, landed in jail for two days, got out and now they came for retribution. It wasn't much of a fight; they just broke a clay flowerpot over my head in front of my mother. What the hell was I thinking? What am I doing? Where am I going?

About this time in 1976 and trying to get my life straight, I met a girl of whom I fell head over heals for and was, for the first time in my life, in love. She was the daughter of a woman who did my mother's nails and her name was Annie. She and I hit it off right from the start and although the relationship was short lived, for a brief period I was changing. I actually began to feel my emotions stir and she brought out the most intellectual person in me. This is when I found it awkward and difficult to express myself and Annie was so loving and understanding she took all my bad dreams and experiences away with a gentle look. She had eyes that healed a soul and mine was in disarray. For once, I looked forward to a bright new day and she changed my outlook and released a beautiful person that I never knew. She saw this in me and it was growing stronger.

We spent time together sharing one another's feelings. At least the ones I would let her into. I think I was about too let her in the most protected feelings I ever considered under lock and key. I trusted her so much and she trusted me.

One exciting day after a hard day's work I gave Annie a phone call and all I remember was that I was excited. I was so excited just to talk to her, listen to her voice, share the day, but her mother answered the phone. I'll never forget that day as her mother began to berate me with obscenities, telling me she doesn't even want me around her daughter, don't call, don't come over, nothing, or she would call the Police. She continued with, I was no good and not good enough for her daughter. That I was "a nothing, a no body and had no reason to be around her daughter".

When I finally hung up the phone, it was the first time in my life that I fell apart and broke down. My mother walked by my room and saw my state and wanted to know what happened, she was shocked at what I told her.

Annie's mother also went so far as to tell Annie, as she was laying in a hospital bed for a nervous condition, to promise her never to see me again for fear she will die. Annie complied. I felt Annie's pain as she told me, knowing she was in conflict with her mother and I was such a wimp at the time and naïve that a parent could do such a thing, so I respected her wishes. I knew I just had to bury this incident deep, where it remained until now. I immediately started using again.

As time went by I kept using and getting into trouble going from one detoxification to another. Seeing doctors who would give me all the drugs I wanted, mainly *seconal.* I ended up in two psychiatric hospitals in the same year, one in the city of Brea and one in Santa Ana. I overdosed at the one in Brea and woke up strapped naked to a bed with leather straps on my wrists, ankles and waist. There were more drugs in there than out in the streets and the one in Santa Ana was a fat farm. I gained so much weight and went to so many sessions, that all I wanted was out of there. They kept asking me, "why are you trying to kill yourself"? In addition, I thought the question was ridiculous. I couldn't find what I was looking for. To quit using on my own. To free myself from this world of self inflicted pain that I was creating. To find peace of mind and just to put my feet out and stop the world. It didn't work that way and if something doesn't happen soon, I'll be dead.

"The Family"
(The First Step)

◆

Loneliness was now a big part of my life. During the short periods of time when I was clean I would visit my old friends and peers, looking for a part of my life that was non existent. I was not the same, they weren't the same. That closeness of friendship that once was, was gone.

The separation took part of me away and the road I chose to take, was a very big mistake. I missed the good times, the good old days, when I had friends who cared about me, who didn't know my secrets and life was just a party. I was good at beating myself up over it and somewhat of an expert in self-pity. I carried this big emotional bag around my neck. To be honest, I didn't know I had it on. At the time, other people could see me better than I could see myself, but I couldn't see it. It was a curiosity, something I needed desperately to awaken and it was coming this way. I was always so negative and allowed my mind to be overcome with self-pity, grief and woes and I couldn't let go of it.

Between getting strung out again, the probation office on my heels, and my will to change, I found a program recommended by "The Methadone Center" and "The Probation Department". It was in the City of Norwalk at the "Metropolitan State Hospital". I was almost 27 and I was going nowhere fast. "So what," I thought, "I got nothing to lose," I said to the counselor at the Methadone Center. They made arrangements to put me on the waiting list. The waiting list was two to three weeks long and sometimes a month.

The trick is, that when you're strung out and have to wait for anything, there is a good chance you will be arrested before you can meet that deadline. Many times the waiting list gets shifted around and many people don't make it. They end up in jail or dead.

While on methadone, a lot of people cheat and use street drugs at the same time, trying to beat the precautions the Center takes, like random urine screenings. It was the Golden Seal days. That's when most street people took an herb called golden seal to give a negative urine test. Sometimes it worked, sometimes not.

The Center called my parent's home to inform me they had a spot for me and when I passed buy, they told me I only had a few minutes to get there. I made it on time, my father made sure of that; he was always good at being on time and instilled it in me.

Five people made the shuttle that day. We headed north on the 5-Freeway towards Los Angeles. We got off on Norwalk Boulevard towards the hospital. All of us were quiet and had heard the stories of frontal lobotomies that took place at Metro State in years passed.

We were waiting to get out and have a cigarette, apprehensive of what was to come. Some were just going to detoxify so when they got out, they didn't have to do as many drugs as they were taking now. Kind of like tapering down. I already tried that and it didn't work, but it's one of those things, that no matter how much you tell someone, they have to try it for themselves.

When we got to the gates, the place looked very old, like it was built in the Thirties. It had a unique style, some Spanish looking buildings with arches and heavy tiles on the roofs; all with wire mesh in the window areas. It had nice areas of garden flowers and grass with benches to sit on. The building we pulled up to was dirty and well used needing a paint job. The sidewalk was full of cracks and grass and weeds were growing out unkempt. We were led in, when a nurse in street clothes came out to check our names.

Inside, the halls were huge with metal doors that led outside echoed loudly. Walking down the hallway were cells with small glass windows in solid steel doors. Women were in them; all sick looking, in various stages of dress. Some had almost nothing on, and the weather was so hot. I recognized one woman, my cousin Margaret from Delhi who was really my cousin Henry's wife. We could only say Hi and were told to move along. She looked really bad and haggard, like it was taking it's toll on her to detox. The two women who rode with us were separated and we placed what belongings we had in the men's dorm. People who looked like street people and dope fiends searched them for contraband. It reminded me of jail and already I wanted to get out. This little thing in the back of my mind told me to stay, besides, I didn't arrange for a ride back and who would want me in my condition.

I kept thinking about Margaret and how she feels. She gave me a look like I was *packing* or if I had any dope on me, I thought to myself. As it turned out, the cells were the women's section. The dorms were for men because there were more men than women.

After they searched our luggage and assigned us to a bed, we were told to go to the dayroom. They called us one by one to fill out papers on, how long we'd been using, how much we'd use in a day. I also took a test, more like a psychological exam. There were questions like, "do you look at your stools in the toilet?" that one was sick so I said no! "Do you count street signs?"

Most of us were already starting to get sick, so I wasn't in the mood for questions. After signing various forms of consent and confidentiality, I was told to go back to the dayroom and wait for my first dose. Waiting is always boring and looking around, everyone else was bored, and it was hot and the fans in the wire mesh windows were too dirty for any air to circulate. Legs were hanging over the chair arms. Tank tops and shorts in disarray. Smoking and the television blaring out sounds no one was listening too. The only thing clean about the place was the floor, it shined bright, but even the floor had cigarette butts on it and there were plenty of ashtrays. It just seemed like nobody gave a shit about nothing, except the next dose.

When the nurses station started calling us, that got some attention as wanting eyes lusted over the dosages being handed out. I drank mine fast and licked the cup before I threw it away. I thought, "what the hell have I got myself into now?" Now that I had my dose and was confident I wasn't going to get sick I went back to the dorm and started to unpack and make conversation. I met one of the persons who had checked my luggage.

"Do you work here?" I asked.

"Sort of, but I'm a patient too".

"What the fuh?" and my thoughts dropped off. "You mean, you are just like us?"

"Yes", he said, "only clean".

Wow, that got my attention and as we continued to talk, I could see myself as doing the same thing he was. My spirits were lifted a bit as I thought about helping others, especially dope fiends. Like always, I put myself outside of myself with mass fantasies and illusions of grandeur. Later, I thought, "what was I thinking? The guy is probably a *rat* anyway".

At dinner, I saw my cousin Margaret and I was glad to see her.

"Where's Henry?"

"Still running the streets and he should be here with me," she said.

She didn't eat much and looked sick, kind of pale and had the sweats. She did think I brought some dope in and looked at me like I was stupid for not doing so.

"Margaret, we came in here to get clean, not see how good we can sleaze through this," I said.

She still looked at me like I was stupid.

"This place was full of rats and that they have a program over here that makes rats out of you," she said.

I didn't understand where she was coming from and let it be. Margaret was a true dope fiend and I knew that some day, it was going to be how she died.

As time passed in the detox ward, which was for one month, I found out that they had another thirty day program, if you wanted to stay and continue your sobriety. While talking to the dope fiend patients who worked there, they told me about it and said it was part of a program called, "The Family". As we talked I always got this impression or sense that they knew what we were all about, like reading your mind or have the ability to see through you. It was a feeling like they could read your thoughts no matter where the thoughts took you. After all, they had been there too, as dope addicts go, but it was really scary and intriguing on the feelings they expressed and how I could relate to them. It looked to me like; maybe they had the answers I was looking for. Like finding wisdom and hope to this maniac world, I created around me. It couldn't hurt to try. Look at where I was at, in a nut house full of people as lost and confused as I was.

Detox was not fun at all. It was miserable and hot and stinky but somehow this time might be the road I'd been looking for. I looked to have possibilities for self-improvement and start a new life. I decided to go over to the thirty-day program. Those, who decided to go over, were only a few. Three individuals convinced me it's for the better, but I wasn't totally sure. I needed to find out for myself. Especially find out what they meant by rats. My interpretation of a rat is a person who snitches on your illegal activities, not one who points out your behavior.

It was from them, the family that I learned about behavior modification and here I was entering into a new realm of exploration of the soul. "Maybe this time," I thought to myself, "Maybe this time."

It was a short walk to the new "Ward", this one was a two-story building and we were headed for the top floor. It was old and as before, all the windows had security screens. The inside was very clean and the furniture was in better shape than where we just came from. The floors shined like glass and we were given rooms, instead of a dorm. There were four persons to a room and closet space. "Wow," I thought, "this is just like a hotel." We joked and called it a country club.

After unpacking, we had an orientation in the dayroom, which was spotless. They placed all the chairs in a circle and we introduced ourselves and became accustomed with the other people on the ward. There were two people who led the whole session and they said they were from the "Family House" and were there to pay back what was given to them. It was strange and I wanted to know more. They told us, that this would be lightweight and not be too heavy on us because we were still feeling the after effects of being drug free. When we didn't feel well, we could be excused from the group and go lay down. That was nice of them, "I wondered what they mean by not being too heavy on us," I thought to myself.

When it came time to eat, we were led downstairs and told no communication with its occupants. The occupants on the lower floor were in a sixty-day program. The food was much better and on Sundays we could sleep in and make our own breakfast when we got up.

The group sessions became more frequent and light. Some people really had some difficult problems and some were just there to clean up just for awhile. I told them, "I was tired of doing dope"

They asked me, "do you really believe that?"

I didn't have an answer, but I said, "yes, I believe that." I wasn't sure, if I believed it or not.

The leader said, "you'll have time to figure that out, but it's going to take more than thirty days."

Her name was Jane and she was somewhat enchanting when she spoke. I guess I was mesmerized at such an intelligent beauty. I was always a sucker for that. She also said, "I hope you give us enough time to get to know you better and decide to go further." She directed that statement to all of us, but like a self-centered fool, I liked to think, she was directing it at me.

They spent long days there on the ward with us. I wondered about how the family was, because these people got here at 6:30 a.m. and didn't leave until 10:30 that evening. Now, I've had some jobs before, but this really must take some dedication to work such long hours and not get paid for it. Could I put myself in such a place to do that?

When we had groups, they told me how they saw me and it was like they knew every aspect of my life. I felt they knew me better than I knew myself. I found out that they did know me better than I knew myself and that was a shocker. I was a lost soul and when I tried to explain my feelings, I found out I had no idea what the concept of feeling was. I was being honest and they even tore that apart telling me,

"How could you be honest if your actions didn't match your intentions".

"Everyone is full of good intentions," they would also say.

I was taught about questioning my own thoughts and ideas. They taught us about their structure on *monads* and *dyads*. A *monad* meaning to be quiet or silence while a dyad being able to talk to another.

We were also told about *haircuts* as a discipline. Not the haircut as to cut your hair, but as to yell at you at the top of our lungs. The *haircut* was a shocker and a wake-up. These were some of the tools used for behavior modification.

They also taught us about the "game" or at least a softer version of it. All chairs, approximately twelve, are arranged in a circle, leaving enough space in between to get in and out. No *acting out* or getting violent allowed; it's immediate cause for dismissal off the property. No communicating outside the game once it starts. You can enter or leave the game anytime you want except during the *carom shot*. That is when all participants are in the game circle and you wish to give someone a game because they want it or because they need it.

With beginners, it's usually because they need it. The *carom shot* may start out with an ambiguous saying that could relate to anyone. "I want to talk to someone in the circle, whose attitude really sucks." By this time, most people know who has been having a bad attitude. Someone else would take the Que and say, "Is this person, by any chance also a slob and don't know how to make a bed?"

So now, we know this person has a bad attitude and is a slob and can't make a bed. The game continues until it lands on an individual. Sometimes it backfires as a smokescreen and lands on someone totally unexpected. A leader, who can call the game at any time, always maintains control. You may leave or enter a game only after the carom shot has made its target individual in the circle. If you leave the circle while inside, you must make tell each person sitting next to you, and verbally tell him or her, "Getting up!" To the left side and "Getting up!" To the right. If someone outside the game wishes to come in, they must tap the back of the person's chair with two loud taps and that person inside must repeat the "getting up sequence".

One of the objectives of the game is break down the individual character armor and get them to feel and explain their behavior. Once broken down and the objective met, all must participate to bring that person up and make sure they are all right. I liked the games, but it was frustrating to me and to the group leaders, because they couldn't figure me out. I had something to hide and I hid it well.

When I was finally backed to a corner, I couldn't come out with it and they thought I was lying. I was taunted because they thought I was in there to hide from a criminal action. Some people were sent to the program from the courts and I told them I would be a volunteer, if anything. They kept at it and at a point, I guess they figured I would not be a good candidate for the "Family House." After that, when we had games again, they talked to me in a lowered tone of voice. Their new approach was quiet and one step at a time.

It was Jane's idea for that approach and she believed me. I was so lost to my feelings and I was sincere about changing my life. I came to believe that this program had what I needed. Somehow in my gut, I knew that if I didn't dump the garbage I was carrying, I would die miserably. At the same time, I didn't have the courage to do it. Would

I find the courage to release the pain I was carrying? Would it help me if I did? Would I trust these people who were in charge here with my innermost secrets? At times I thought I was going insane and losing my mind. It was a feeling of helplessness I couldn't explain. If I tried, it came out all wrong. What I was hiding would come out in vomit and expose the scared little kid I was trying to protect. Not knowing it then, I had stopped growing emotionally at the age of eight years old. I thought I was retarded and in some ways I was because I had become a slow learner. I was confused; yet, this is the closest I've been in my life to making any sense out of it.

"Do it Mario" a voice said, in my mind.

"Great, now I'm talking to myself" I said out loud.

On about the twenty-eighth day they took me to the "Family House" for my entrance evaluation. It was a long walk and I was blindfolded. On the way they explained the rules again, no violence, no acting out violently, no outside contact for thirty days, no personal clothing. Only state clothing could be worn for thirty days and if accepted and I agreed I would shave my head bald. Being baldheaded during this period in time was not the in thing to do. It was considered offensive and demeaning. Only nut cases were baldheaded and it was the "Families" way to strip character and slowly rebuild it. This was a one to two-year program and in some cases, longer.

At the Family House, I was told to sit on, "*the bench*." I heard music playing until I sat down, then the music stopped and the entire house got quiet. They took off the blindfold and reminded me not to communicate to anyone. Above the bench was a sign I was told to read. It went something like this, "When you feel that everything is going against you and you cannot hold on for one minute more, never give up then, for that is just the time and the place when the tide will turn". "What am I getting myself into," I thought.

Now, at the time, the family was one of the hardest programs in the United States to complete. In fact, it was one of the only programs in the

United States. It also had the highest success rate for drug recovery and it was protected and governed by it's own people. I had thoughts of it being a cult.

"Mario," I heard someone say.

I looked up and it was one of the friends from the Detox Ward.

"You can get up now and follow me."

I was lead down a hallway and all was quiet. The people in the living room would not stare at me. In fact, they ignored me and kept doing whatever they were doing, only silently. She led me to a set of double doors and led me in.

In the room was a set of bleachers where approximately twelve people were sitting. In front was a single chair facing them. I was told to sit in the chair. One person was wearing a cardboard sign, saying something about always being late on it. There were equally men, and women, one of whom I recognized from the detox center. She smiled at me and it was reassuring, like everything was going to be ok.

All these people were ex-dope fiends in recovery and in different stages of the program, but all were experienced enough to do evaluations. I was about to experience something way out of the ordinary and somewhat bizarre.

"Are you ready?" the speaker asked. "Because if your not, you can go right back to the ward".

"No, no, I'm ready" I said.

It seemed like they could care less if I was there or not. Like I was interrupting something more important.

"Mario, do you know why you're here?" she asked.

"Yes, to get clean."

That must have been the wrong answer, because the next thing that happened totally took me by surprise at the strength and force with which it was delivered. All of them at once began yelling at me from the top of their lungs in a cacophony of noise and voices. I swear my hair was blowing backwards.

"You stupid son of a bitch, don't you know you're here to save your life?" someone yelled.

At the same time another saying, "Don't you know that other people could be here, who want to live?"

"Who let this guy in here? Get rid of him!" Another voice yelled.

Still another, "You gotta a lotta balls coming in here with that bullshit!"

They just yelled and yelled and as they yelled, I could see pain coming out of their mouths. Pain backed by experience. Feelings that I myself was unable to express and it was all happening at once, like one big giant pulse of information going right through me. I couldn't grasp one single piece of it.

My mind went on instant overload and I sat there with my jaw dropped, like a dummy in a trance, awestruck at what just took place. If ever there was a picture of stupidity, I was it. These guys were the "heavy hitters", the "big guns" as the sayings go.

"What's your story?" one of them asked from the left.

I must have looked sorry to them.

"Why are you here?" another said.

"Are you running from the law?" said a voice from the right.

I just "*dummied up*" and couldn't get anything out. When I tried to speak, it came out a stutter and I couldn't believe what was happening. I was cut short when I did try to answer. They were deliberately trying to frustrate me, only everyone knew it but me.

After it quieted down and they seemed friendlier.

I was asked, in a low tone of voice, "Mario, why do you use drugs?"

I smiled now, because I knew the answer to this one.

"Because I like them" was the answer.

Wrong! They all started yelling at me with a force louder than before. If ever before I was confused, it sure was now. I was dizzy with it. My head started to hurt. I felt like walking out on them, but I knew, no matter what, I was going to see this through. It lasted almost an hour and a half, one of the longest evaluations in their record as I found out later. I'm sure I frustrated them also and I don't think they knew what to do with me.

They sent me back out on the *bench* to wait. While I was sitting, more people came and there was lots of talking going on. I figured it was about me and thought, maybe I should just get up and leave. Then I looked at the sign again at the part where it says to "never give up then."

They called me in again. There were different people in there and one was the chief. He asked questions concerning people out to get me and if I was hiding from them.

"Why do you want to volunteer to stay here on your own without being prodded by the courts?" he asked.

"Because I would be willing to give up a year of my life if it was going to benefit me, for the rest of my life.

"OK, How do you think we can help you?"

"By showing me how I can become a better person and to be drug free". It was the most sincere voice I could muster.

"Do you need help?"

"Yes, I need help" I said with a sigh! "I need lots of help," I said again.

"Good! He said, because you are going to have to convince us you need help. I want you to get on the floor and tell us you need help, I want to hear it with all you got from the top of your lungs".

I swallowed hard and my mind was racing with thoughts of trust. "Could I trust them with making a fool of myself in front of them? "God, this is so embarrassing," I knew I needed help, but this, I didn't want to do it. It must have shown on my face because one of the girls, Jane, from the other ward started talking. She assured me that it was no big thing to do, but it is something I must do.

"We need to know if you're sincere," she said.

I got on my knees and yelled, "I need help!"

"Louder!" they all yelled as if cheering me on.

"I need help!" I yelled again.

"Louder, say it like you mean it!" they yelled."

"I need all the help I can get!" I finally yelled.

That seemed to satisfy them and the tone dropped and they talked softly now. The chief asked me to go back outside and sit on the *bench*.

While I was sitting, my mind was racing, spinning and I really didn't know what to think. I had just been through an experience I never thought possible or existed. "What if they laugh at me," I thought, "what would I do?"

After a few minutes, I was called back in. They were smiling now and welcomed me.

"You made it," they said.

They all came off the bleachers and started congratulating me and giving me hugs. I was uneasy getting hugs from the men. This was a new experience for me and my world was about to change. I was about to find out about unconditional love.

We went over a few more rules, like shaving my head, wearing state clothes, and wearing two wristbands, one saying "FEEL" and the other "SELF-WORTH." These were the concepts I had to work on during my stay. This may sound funny to you, but I had absolutely no idea what a concept was. The words had little meaning to me.

I had doubts about making the thirty-day period that it took to get my street clothes back. I also knew that if I just stuck with it I could make it work.

I started at the bottom of the totem pole, so to speak. They gave me a job doing kitchen cleanup every day. You had to hurry and clean tables, sweep, mop, wash dishes and be ready for the next meeting or session within a few minutes. I was constantly being hurried, stopped and given a *haircut*.

I dreaded the evening meeting because I knew I was going to have to stand up and speak to the group about my concepts. By the time I reached the meeting and stood up to talk about my concepts, I couldn't talk. Nothing came out and they had to say, "sit down!" I couldn't come up with what I thought they wanted to hear. Later I found out that, was wrong. Every day was hell for me and they mentally prodded, probed, yelled at me. I was given *haircut* after *haircut*. I sat in a corner with a toothbrush, polishing a single floor tile for eight hours a day dwelling in self-pity.

I was assigned a "Tribe Leader" by the name of Jeff. He and the tribe worked with me day and night. He tried everything on me because of his experience. Jeff was good at what he did. I guess they figured that if any body could help me, it would be Jeff.

They kept on trying to break me and because of my attitude of self-pity, along with the inner child trying to hide from the demons, they told me I had to wear a diaper for days. I wore it and it was humiliating. Can you imagine a grown man in a diaper? I was almost to a point for some serious ass kicking and I had thoughts of leaving, but also knew this was what I asked for. Jeff even talked to me by candlelight, trying to get me to feel. I thought I was doing fine, but what I thought was fine and what they thought was fine are two totally different things. I was a dummy to them, but I was as honest as I could be.

I kept getting the games put on me and they would try and tear my character armor down. As Jeff once said,

"It's like tearing you down, just to bring you up, like molding a clay sculpture."

It was the way they perceived it. An analogy was a better way for me to understand.

Whenever I thought they were getting close to my past as a child, I got around it somehow changing the subject or putting the session off on someone else. I would never go there and it was eating me alive. I just knew I would be embarrassed and humiliated. This was the way I thought and my way of thinking was seriously damaged.

It took ninety days to get my clothes back, the longest on record.

After countless meetings and not being able to talk about how I felt, it came out one day. Of course, I was well programmed by then and knew how to skirt subjects and project my feelings, which really weren't mine, but a projection of another's that were similar. It was the first time I wasn't told to sit down. I expressed how tired I was getting at not being able to talk.

"That's what we've been trying to get you to express." Jeff said.

"It is?" Still not being sure what had just happened.

The constant group sessions and therapy I received helped me to come out of a shell and construct positive thoughts, ideas, contribute to the sessions, even control my emotions to a point. I was changed from a quiet, shy, individual to outgoing, authoritative with no fear of expression. In fact, I think I learned to talk too much, but it was new and felt good. I also liked the hugs; I got lots of hugs. They taught me to hug and from this, I learned to hug my father, which was something I had not done since I was a child before the trauma. I actually thought I found the thing that would make my life better and out of the life of drugs. For a time, it was great to be alive again and to be able to see a clear future, like finding a magical place where everything is at peace.

The only thing that I found about the program that was wrong was the fact that they didn't like you to go to church.

"Why do you want to go to church now, you didn't go when you were running around all crazy in the streets, did you?" they would say.

It struck hard and I never expressed my feelings toward the church to them. Although I despised the church for what it did to me, I also forgave them and I keep that feeling going.

It was only a matter of time that I began to change again, only worse than before. I was never able to just, come out with it. I wanted to, I really wanted to, but who could talk about being molested and humiliated, carrying the pain for years, the disgust and self-loathing that comes with it? How, when it came to a decision between right and wrong, wrong would always take precedence for fear of looking bad? Having a bad case of winning everyone's approval no matter what the consequences were? It was this, not giving in to my deepest feelings of pain, anguish, disgust, and suffering that allowed my mind to become overcome with negative thoughts. I could have just surrendered, but at the time, I couldn't see it and was blind to the truth. It was my downfall from grace with the family.

After I got my street clothes back, I worked the "*Detox* Ward" on the evening shift with people who were still suffering and sick. There were some people there I knew from the streets. After some talk of the old days, I let them out to go to the liquor store and buy a bottle to take the edge off the kicking stage. They weren't going to leave or get drugs to bring in, just some liquor. It was a very bad decision and again, I allowed myself to please, instead of saying "no."

When they got back and got high, they left bottles under the beds, to which the next crew found. I was awakened by a tribe leader and the Chief and told to sit on the *bench*. There was a hearing going on and I knew what it was about. The morning crew found liquor bottles under the beds in the Detox Ward. They asked questions about knowing anything and there were three of us involved. I didn't want to play dumb and didn't want the others to be punished for my offense so I just came out with it. I told them, the responsibility was mine and apologized for my indiscretion. The discipline they offered was not to my liking, so I told them, it was time to go and I split.

I was there for 11 months of the most intensive training imaginable. I signed the release papers and felt a lump in my throat. As I walked out the door, luggage in hand, head up, and not turning around, I could feel the mistake I made and convinced myself, that it's OK. I kept trying to tell myself I could do it. When I looked around, I knew I couldn't, without the support of the others, alone. "No one ever makes it alone," I thought. They taught self-reliance without faith and the two needed each other.

"Unfolded Reality"
(mi vida loca)
(my crazy life)

◆

In less than 12 hours, I was back *in the spoon*. I had enough to buy a car and I meant well, but I just had to do it. It was a very compulsive strong feeling, like I wanted it to go away or disappear, but it wouldn't. It was like a big chunk of my soul had been discarded. I knew that back at the Family House all the friends I had made were going through turmoil because of me. When someone splits, the entire House takes it out on itself.

In my case, I was the little brother who ran away. Now they had to pay for it for not catching on as to why. They were now suffering what is called, "Shaking the Tree" A ritual of disciplines for 18 hours. I knew the whole house was on a *monad*, scrubbing windows, mopping, waxing, and getting *haircuts* in a rage. They tried to find out if anyone else wanted to split.

Afterwards, candlelight encounters experiencing grief and loss. The loss was I and to them, I had died when I walked out. They would do this until the wounds healed and were sure all was ok again.

I also had to use more of the drug than usual. People said it was because I had uncovered my feelings and it takes a lot more drugs to cover them up.

Covering them up can lead to very dangerous situations, like an overdose. You hear about people overdosing, trying to get that first *rush* again. But it never comes. The only "*rush*" you get is death and your spirit goes out of you, just as happy as can be, feeling no pain. It's when your friends get scared and try to bring you back. In a panic, they beat you and slap you to come out of it. Put you in ice cold water in the tub and put ice under your balls. You would think that would be enough to wake you, but the drug is very powerful. I woke up many a time, black and blue from an overdose. Sore all over from the beatings and the only thing I could think of was "where is my dope?" From one dope fiend to another Sorry! When you're out, there's nothing more anyone can do. Your dope is gone! If you survived to get back at your friends, they always said,

"I thought you were dead" and to them I was dead.

There was one time I overdosed and thought I died because as they had me on a gurney at UCI medical center rushing me in, I couldn't respond or move my body. Although I could clearly hear everything the doctors and nurses were saying and I could feel the cold air, nothing worked. I could not move my arms, open my eyes, move my head, nothing! My body was dead as far as the hospital staff was concerned.

"He's not going to make it." I heard a male doctor say.

That's all it took because with all the strength I could muster, I shook violently and came out of it and my heart started beating again.

People say that when you die, there is a moment when you can see the people around you from an angle just above the body, but you can't communicate. I thought I was in that place, between two worlds, where I could have given up the ghost or stayed to endure the pain of living. I wasn't living, and the world I created around me was just, an existence.

After I did wake and leave the hospital after 72 hours, I thought to myself, "why didn't I just die and get it over with?" It came to me that I was scared, too scared to die and too scared to live. I was a mess. I also thought, "maybe God had a purpose for all this, maybe it's just not my time to go and some day I'll find the answer?" These were just moments when I was thinking sanely.

But that's all it was, just moments, because as soon as I got released, I went out for another fix. I threw all the experience down the drain and instead of heeding to the learning process, I continued down the dark path of misery and pain. I kept on pushing into darkness, keeping company with the most ruthless people you could imagine. Learning the dark ways of theft, running from police, going in and out of jails and institutions, scamming the innocent, and doing whatever it takes to get the next fix. Without getting busted. It is inevitable that if you are going to live this life, you are going to get busted and the odds are against you.

I was arrested for burglary and sent back to prison for another three years. This time I was burglarizing a house in South Santa Ana. I had a small pick-up truck and after *scoping* a neighborhood, I picked the house most convenient. I backed up boldly in the driveway, put my wallet in the glove box, just in case I lost it, and walked to the front door. The door was exposed to the street, so I had to make it fast. Once in I quickly scanned the inside for anything of expense.

I had a gut feeling about this and knew I had to hurry, so I started on the stereo equipment. Disconnecting every wire I could find and loading speakers rapidly into the truck. I was almost complete, when the homeowners came home and parked directly in front of my truck blocking me in.

I came out, still with the stereo receiver in my hands when an old man with a *gardeners hook*, took a swing at me and almost got my face. I didn't even drop the receiver, but dodged him, put the receiver in the back of the truck and closed it.

I jumped in the front of the truck, started it, and gave it the gun. Unfortunately the transmission was too weak to push the car aside and it started to smoke like the Fourth of July.

I heard yelling, "I called the police" in a frantic tone.

I knew it was time to go. Just as I got out of the truck, the police were rounding the corner and I ran and jumped the fence leading into the back yard of the residence I had just broken into. I had time, I thought, and stayed close knowing the police would think I had gotten farther away. In the backyard, I jumped the neighbors' fence and there was a culdesac. I crossed the culdesac and spotted bushes across the way with just enough cover for me to hide and not quite enough for them to suspect anyone could hide there.

I took the chance and waited silently, every bone in my body ready. My adrenaline was pumping hard like a high, the high pulsing with fear, on instinct and anticipation of the next move. It was cat and mouse now, but I just had to do it, just to see who was better, them or me. My heart beating, ears tuned to every sound and I knew they were near and coming.

I could see two squad cars coming from around the bend I had just come from, lights out, rolling quietly. Across the street from me, two officers got out and started to search the bushes slowly with flashlights. I could see them in an opposite arc from me and they were coming closer.

"Damn!" I muttered, knowing they would be on me in a matter of seconds.

Just before they got to me, and it was about ten feet, I was counting how fast I could get up, split right and jump another fence. Another police car came up, distracted, and told the officers they had just spotted me a few blocks over. For the moment I was relieved, but it wasn't over, I knew I was already busted but had to prolong the run as long as I could. I remembered I had left my wallet in the glove box and it had money in it, so what did I do? I worked my way around the neighborhood where I could get a line of sight back to where my truck was.

I ended up on the porch of a house with good cover and I could see the activity going on to where my truck was. It was cold now and I was getting tired of this, I knew I was busted and it was a matter of time, but did they get my wallet? I had to know. If they did, they probably were thinking, this was the stupidest burglar they ever caught. I couldn't tell and saw the tow truck hooking up my truck to the back and thought, just as he turns the corner I could jump on and get my wallet back.

I was ready, and my heart started to pound at the unthinkable thing I was about to do. I saw the tow truck driver get in the truck and I was ready. He made a U-turn in the opposite direction and it blew my whole trip. ARRRGH! I wanted to scream at the stupid thing I just did. I waited until it was clear before I proceeded my next move.

I had cousins close by so I worked my way toward their house knowing I could stay there for the night. I walked and ran for miles dodging every car, sound, and light that even got close to me. I was like an animal, traveling on pure instinct, just like in the movie; "Altered States" survival was the game now. And to what end? Only to postpone time and get one more fix before I went back to jail.

In the morning at my cousins in the back house, which was well secured, the parole officers came in like a Swat Team. They saw that it was locked from the inside and started breaking down the door to where I was. Not before I got one last fix before they broke through. It happened so fast. They were pounding on sealed windows and the fortified door. I was loaded before they got me with the needle still in my arm.

As I was handcuffed, I said, "Hey! You got a cigarette?"

Just to piss them off.

*   *   *

It surely is a good thing we have a system to put those of us away who need it. This may sound harsh, especially if you're the one who needs to be put away and it does give one time to think about consequences. It does give us "clean time". People in jail would say, "you got saved" when you got busted, but they meant saved from the streets and from yourself. For some, it's just enough time to go back and use again, and it was deliberate. I didn't think that way. I believed that some day I would be able to be clean. Only when I was put up against self-motivation, that motivation would lose, because the odds were against us.

The last time I was released, I told the parole people I would make it.

"I'll give you a week or I'll give you ninety days max." was their response.

There was no hope in the message. It was the same, with the people from the California Department of Corrections.

"You'll be back," they would say.

I couldn't believe how many addicts really believed that they did feel better if they just cut out all hope, then they would have a basis to say, "*mi vida loca.*" It was what was called, "the revolving door syndrome," in and out of jail. I have been busted, got out and less than three hours, back in again.

This time back in prison, I was sent back to "Sierra Conservation Center", a center for training fire fighters. This was a camp scene for low risk, minimum security inmates only, usually ones who just have drug offenses and others who are coming out of a higher security and are on their last three years before parole release. We trained for the "California Department of Forestry" and were sent to camps throughout California.

I got to see more of California and the beautiful countryside than I ever did in the streets. The training gave us a sense of responsibility and a chance to prove ourselves to ourselves. It was a test against strength and stamina. Rigorous training and sometimes in difficult situations like working in freezing cold with a minimum of protection or in blazing heat, enough to singe your eyebrows. Also, working the fires with a crew of twelve, cutting fire line at breakneck speed, watching for spot fires jumping the line you just cut and the smoke fillings your lungs. I would light a cigarette in the densest of smoke at break time. The food was good during a fire and we got extra pay, not much, but it was extra. Enough to buy your own coffee and cigarettes for the next month.

I went to a camp in northern California called "Black Mountain". It was nestled in the mountains about ninety miles north of San Francisco and very close to the coast amongst the redwoods near a town called "Guerneville". It was the most beautiful spot on the face of the earth. The local deer population would come into camp looking for handouts of cookies or whatever they could get.

The crews would go out daily mostly clearing debris from river channels or outlets to the ocean during the winter months. The jobs were always dangerous and we had two deaths in one crew that was working at the ocean, clearing debris from a cove. While eating lunch on the rocks near the edge, the ocean swelled and swallowed the two, dragging them out to sea. No one could get close to them. One tried and broke his leg in the crags of the rocks. I went with the lieutenant to pick him up and take him to San Quentin Prison for medical care. The other two were not removed until two days later when the ocean swells were more forgiving.

We also had another inmate injured while cutting fire line. He was *bucking* logs and the chainsaw *bucked back*, hitting him in the face. Luckily, his helmet visor, which is made of plastic, slowed the chain down, but it did cut him right down the middle, cutting his nose in half and lips in half, leaving marks on his forehead and chin which were cut to the bone. And he was lucky! A helicopter landed in camp and took him to a nearby hospital. I had to hand it to these guys, it was dangerous out on the line and I was safe in camp. Sometimes I think the good lord put me in these situations, but it wasn't always safe.

I stayed in camp working in the kitchen as extra help. I had a good paying job and kept busy doing work no one else liked to do. It was funny because instead of peeling potatoes, they just ran them through the French fry cutter. The blades of the cutter were full of maggots when I first saw it. I took it apart and went to work, cleaned it, steamed it, and oiled it. I actually came in early peeled all the potatoes and blanched them before dinner. That way, when the crews came in, the French fries cooked to a golden brown in a matter of seconds were hot off the fryer, salted, served and very tasty.

The crews noticed changes as soon as I started working the kitchen. On my free time I was cutting redwood burl and making tables, lamps, and clocks, sending them home for sale and making extra money. Although all our immediate needs were met, living on two dollars and thirty cents a day was difficult if you smoked and drank coffee, or wanted extras, like equipment or supplies to work with. I was grateful for just the chance to do so.

The camp lieutenant was a motivating element to the inmates and treated us with mutual respect. He even let us keep a wild boar he encountered in the rode, so the kitchen crew raised him and kept him out of trouble. I also learned how to make belt buckles and, with the help of the lieutenant and the first cook, make smoking pipes, made out of deer antler and abalone shells. Some magnificent pieces were made at that camp.

There was tension in the camp because some of the kitchen supplies were being used to make "*pruno*". This was only for select "Skinhead" type few. So when the crews began getting less and less of their rations, like sugar, fruits, jellies and jams the tension became intense and it all fell on the kitchen crew which was "White Supremacist" orientated. They offered to share with me, but only to keep me quiet and I couldn't handle that.

One day while the crews were coming in for breakfast I put out an extra can of jelly to make sandwiches and the crews responded with a shock and surprise and at the same time one of the cooks got really pissed and tried to take it back. I grabbed it from his hands and put it back on the serving table. The "Correctional Officer" on duty didn't have a clue as to what was going on, but the rest of the population knew what was happening and were on my side.

Later in the morning during cleanup routine, the cook threatened to hurt me while holding a big knife, a very big knife.

I yelled at him telling him from the dinning area,

"It ain't right what you're doing. Give it your best shot, I'm right here, besides that stuff belongs to them, not you."

He turned red and you could see the veins popping out of the side of his neck. A few of the others were watching to see what his reaction was going to be.

"One of us is going to have to move," he said in an angry voice.

"You got that right! You!" I retorted, still holding the mop handle in my hands ready for action. The others were smirking now.

He slammed the knife in the sink and muttered, "We'll see!" as he walked out of the kitchen.

"Yea, we'll see," I muttered in mocking as I returned to mopping the floor.

In the afternoon when the crews arrived, I was a hero and word traveled fast in a small camp of eighty men. After that, the cook didn't even look my way and he was there on a trial basis. He transferred the following week to another camp and the lieutenant made an excuse for him to have an honorable retreat.

I was mostly a loner during the day and stayed away from the gangs just because I knew it was more trouble than it was worth. I wasn't about to prolong a short sentence.

I continued working on my off time with a friend, Sonny from Orange County. He and I had a mutual understanding and plans for the future. I learned what I could and got out, but I still did stupid things.

I had gotten married to my first wife back at Sierra and when she came up for a *bone-yard visit*, she brought the drugs and alcohol I had encouraged her to bring. The visit was farther north at another campsite called "Parlin Fork". She came late, very late and she was supposed to be there at 1:00 p.m. Around 9:00 p.m. in the evening when she got there, she was *out of it*. When we unloaded the groceries, she had a bottle of booze in a grocery bag. Right on top, where anyone could see.

I got *rolled up* and sent to the county jail in the city of Roseville in Placer County. I signed an affidavit stating it was my responsibility and

I told my wife to bring the stuff, otherwise, she would have been arrested also.

Now, I was in a county jail way out of my territory. In the prison system, there are gangs and there are gangs. This far north, were what is called, "*the nortenos*," I was from the south and an enemy even if I wasn't in a gang. They didn't know I wasn't in a gang, they just knew I was from the south and I was ready for action of some type.

Now, to be in the prison system, you have to be a good navigator because it has many twists and turns. I considered myself as a good navigator.

After being booked in and led upstairs to my cell, it was very late, about three a.m. In the cell were seven inmates and I was eight. There was one bunk open made of solid steel and another inmate had taken the bedroll from that bunk and was asleep. Now, the dilemma was do I wake him and take the bunk roll? Do I knock him out of his bunk? Do I want to make waves knowing I was in bad territory?

"Get off the roll," I said as I shook the guy.

He mumbled something, turned to go back to sleep and I grabbed him.

"That's my roll, give it up." I said.

I hate acting tough, but it worked. It also showed them I was no punk and could stand for my own.

In the morning at *chow,* I got a lot of stares and *vatos* were strolling without shirts, so I could see their northern tattoos trying to intimidate me. It didn't work because I already had it in me that we were going to thump. If I was going to go down, I was going to take somebody with me.

It was all in a look, called *mad-dogging.* I think I got respect because of the night before, because of my size and the fact that I was only going to be there for three days. I knew size could have been a factor but not likely, because I knew already that it's them little guys you have to watch out for. They always carry knives and are fast. It's an old saying, "watch your back", but unfortunately true. . The bus came to take two others and me back to Sierra Conservation Center for my disciplinary hearing.

Back at Sierra, I was given six months loss of privileges and given a job in the boiler room. I learned about making hot water on a large scale and refit many pipes, fittings and cleaned out the boilers. I might as well have been a coal miner because although the boilers were huge, they only had a tiny porthole to crawl through and it took all I had to get into one.

After the six months, I was sent to another camp near Sacramento where I was released to parole. As before, they couldn't wait to get rid of me and treated me like a returning customer and like I was taking them out of their way. It wasn't a good feeling. The releasing Officer left me at a bus stop in the middle of nowhere in the Forrest. I sat on the bench for awhile, took a deep breath of air, and waited.

The smell of the pines does things to you, pleasing things, relaxing. The bus came very soon and broke the silence; reality was giving me another chance or was it? At least they had there timing right I muttered to myself as I got on the bus for Sacramento Airport.

I flew back to "Orange County" with a big whopping two hundred dollars to make it in the world. The flight took almost half of it and the meal I had at the airport was expensive. I met my first wife again, who came down from Santa Barbara in a rented car. I could immediately tell that something was amiss and she had changed because she had this air of paranoia and a far off look in her eyes that avoided contact.

We stayed for a day, then left for Santa Barbara to her apartment. Once in the apartment, I had to look around and could immediately see things were not right. I peeked in the closet and saw men's clothing. My heart sank that I could be so stupid. I confronted her and she assured me nothing was wrong, and that the clothes belonged to her cousin. The thought of her and a cousin together was putrefying to me. I put it out of my mind for the moment thinking I must have been away too long. I stayed the night and had many ideas of finding a new job in a new location, starting over. "Maybe it would work," I thought.

The next day she kept telling me she thought she was pregnant from the night before.

I said, "Whoa! Back up just a minute here".

After she kept telling me, we were going to have a baby. I told her that the letters I sent, must have been some really powerful letters because I never heard of anyone getting pregnant through the mail.

Reality was starting to set in when I realized why she was so late for the visit back at camp. She deliberately sabotaged it by putting the booze on top of the groceries. She had already been with someone else. What did I expect?

After some probing and prodding, she admitted her mistake, which was all I wanted to hear. As it turned out, she was three months pregnant, afraid of being discovered and in between a rock and a hard place. After some lengthy talking, we both knew it wasn't going to work. I just couldn't stand the thought of her and a cousin, which was now, a distant cousin. I did still have love for her and it will always remain, but we were two dope addicts pulling each other down and apart.

We had a dream of being married in "Mission Santa Barbara". Since both of us had "Chumash Indian" ancestry we were allowed access to be married there. Although our dreams seemed so real, it was a bad day for us Indians and the decision we both made of good intentions was only temporary.

We had a party to celebrate our upcoming divorce and to remain friends. On the way home I could see the relief on her face and body. I wondered how the baby would come out?

Back in Santa Ana, I lived with my parents and worked in the garage. I wanted to start a business for myself. I earned a living making tables, clocks, and lamps from the burl collected from the Black Mountain camp. I had help from a friend, Sonny, who was a *swamper* on a crew at the same camp. We previously made an agreement that if I got out first, I would look him up and if he got out first, he would look me up. Well, he got out first and couldn't reach me, so I looked him up and said, "are you ready?"

He had all the wood both of us had sent home and stored. We cleaned out my father's garage and went to work. The wood only lasted the summer and we even put a few more people to work. Some of the sets sold for eighteen hundred dollars, so we weren't doing all bad.

After The wood ran out, I went on my own and started up a jewelry cleaning stand at the Santa Ana Swap Meet. About this time, I met Joanie who is now my wife. We met at a dance in the city of Westminster and stuck together like glue ever since. She came from a family of nine on the Westside of Santa Ana. She had one brother and five sisters so she grew up rivaling her sisters and had a good nature.

She knew I did drugs and I didn't hide it from her. She always insisted that it was my business and she wouldn't get in the way of it. That was fine with me, cause I didn't want to hear any moaning or groaning and she gave me all the rope I wanted. Sometimes I think it really wasn't a good decision. It worked for me and gave me time to think it through. Joanie has seen the drug life from her friends and family also and was not totally naïve to it. She encouraged me to succeed in what ever I wanted although it may have been wrong. I saw strength in her and I needed some of that.

She worked at a factory for twelve years where they made bullets and links for machine guns used in the Viet Nam conflict. I told her that was fine with me, just don't make one with my name on it. Joanie helped me at the Swap Meet on the weekends and it took off. I also started repairing jewelry with the help of library books and the little money I made, I started to build a business.

Business kept me out of trouble, for awhile, and I started to use again. I went on a methadone program and could just make enough money to keep me honest and stay out of trouble.

I spent the weekdays working about twelve hours a day building custom belt buckles and custom wrist bands. I experimented with silver and gold. It's much easier to work the soft metals and soon found out how to make rings and earrings. I did build a nice inventory, but not enough money to get ahead. It got to a point to where I had to return to work on a regular job thinking I could work that and the Swap Meet on the weekends. I worked at the bullet factory with Joanie for awhile, but I didn't like it and the methadone I was on was making me do really stupid things and acting the clown.

It was 1983 and I went back to work at National Technology and Joanie and I had a baby on the way. I was afraid to work there, but I really didn't have a choice. It was the only job I knew how to do well. It was minimum wage, but steady. I always had minimum wage dead end jobs and as before, it just became a means to support my habit.

I was able to work on the side and I would buy silver to make ornaments and jewelry sales were slow. They were slow because it took many hours just to make one piece of jewelry and people at swap meets didn't want to pay what you put into it. I accumulated quite an inventory and sold stuff out of the back of my car. It got old real quick, so I got some help from my insurance to cover a detoxification and entered the "Care Unit" in the city of Orange. I needed help and I knew it. I knew that if I didn't get it right, I would end up back in jail.

In the Care Unit, I detoxed, but this one was different. It wasn't the usual low-income detoxification center. This had upscale individuals with lots of money and fancy cars. There were some famous people in there so I won't break their anonymity. They had food accessible anytime of day and food goodies for night snacks in the fridge. We had regular group sessions and could leave if you weren't feeling well. From the places I have been before, this was a true countryclub. I spoke in front of groups and practically ran the sessions. It was easy navigation through this maze of ritzy people and I was a character, who humored everyone and kept it going with excitement and laughs. Inside, I was shaking, waiting for the moment that I could reveal myself and bare my soul without fear of retribution or humiliation.

The staff was exceptional and took an interest in me. One of the staff was an old friend from the Saunder's, that got messed up in Viet Nam. He was trying to get his life back together and was now doing much better convalescing himself.

I got a referral to see a shrink after my release. He was a clinical psychologist by the name of Mark and we talked several times, just to acquaint myself with him and build some trust. I knew in my mind that I was ready. Ready to tell someone about the pain, I'd been carrying and ready to let someone into my life so that I could begin a change. At this point, I hadn't even told my wife as Joanie and I were married now. She's always been my driving force and encouraged me to do what is right.

I was scared and did everything I was supposed to do. In about the fourth or fifth session, I told him about the molestation and how I'd held it in for all these years. I told him about how the drugs eased the pain and the side effects of using. The overdoses and loneliness I created. How I pushed people away from me and kept myself a loner in fear of being discovered. How I feared this moment and the ridicule.

"No one is going to laugh at you," he said.

I smiled, but I was still tense and not thoroughly convinced this was the right thing to do.

We pushed further and talked of family and friends and hatred and self-loathing. How just to drive here took an act of grace, because the steering wheel in my car had a mind of it's own when pressured. I was lucky I was there in the session, instead of across town at the connections.

"What would you do, if you confronted the person who molested you"? He asked.

"I would beat the f__k out of him and try to break every bone in his body!"

"Would you grind him into the ground?" he said.

"Yes, I would, I would pulverize him and mash him into the cement until there was no more that I could see."

I was crying like a little kid and in some ways, I was a little kid. An emotionally stunted kid in a man's body, with a big open wound in my chest, festering with guilt, shame, and remorse.

He told me that I needed to share this with my family so we set up a meeting. My mother and my sister Cathy came to the meeting. My father didn't want anything to do with it. I knew he was afraid the end result would fall on him and that he would be the blame. Blame wasn't what I was looking for. I forgave my father, because he is from another time and believed in his ways. Just to meet on equal ground would do and for him to see my views on what happened.

Once before, we had a falling out and I told him that my drug use was not his fault. I lied to him, just to make him feel better. To me it was his fault. Not that I was molested, but the fact that he told me, "talk to no one about this" and I still hear it in my head. I do think that if I were better taken care of with more personal and individualized therapy, I wouldn't be in this mess now, wondering what my life had drawn until now, nothing but pain and suffering. I was tired of it and I wanted a new life, and I wanted it now. How many more kids have to suffer need-lessly and how many more are there? I needed to tell my father this, but he wouldn't listen and shut me out if I even got close to the subject.

In the session, it took awhile for me to come out for the second time. I was still confused from the first time and I really didn't get the relief I had expected. I still hurt and was afraid to open the wound again. I knew I had to do this if I was going to live at all.

When I explained it to them, my sister looked at my mother and said, "I never knew" all the time crying and making me cry. Then her life began to fall together,

"No wonder mom always had me take you with me when you were little. I hated you for it," she said.

She told me she was sorry and after it all came out into the light, we all cried together. This was a first step for me and I had high hopes, but like all my life before me, something went wrong.

*   *   *

I kept this wounded feeling in my gut, like I wanted to vomit but couldn't and I needed constant attention after that session. I didn't get it after the bills started to arrive. I thought it was all covered by the insurance. It wasn't and I couldn't afford what they wanted. I made appointments but did not have the strength to return. I know now that I should have gone back in at that time, but none of us knew what chain of events was about to happen. It got worse and I couldn't see the doctor, because he was out of reach all of a sudden. I lost all self-control and my compulsive behavior was way out of control. When I called to make an appointment, he was out and couldn't be reached, when I did make an appointment, something happened and I didn't make it in. Always something got in the way.

I took a lot of drugs trying to cover the intense feelings I was having and I was a time bomb about to explode. It was like I was running, running from the truth, running from myself, running from pain. I continued using and at times ended up in the streets, washing windows at gas stations, anything for money to get high. I even used my hooker friends taking them from one trick to another and sharing a fix from the profits.

I took them to a bar one evening, a rough looking place with mostly Mexican clientele. We sat at the bar, ordered a beer and in less than a minute guys would ask me, how much. I told them to talk to the girls and they would let me know when they went outside with a trick and when they came back.

This night one of the girls, I call "Gangster", came in and was worried about a trick outside, so I went outside to investigate. The client was not satisfied with the results and upset.

I told him, "it's over man, you got your time and that's it".

He pulled a knife on me and told me in Spanish, he was going to stick it in me. I wrapped my jacket on my left arm and crouched; leaning forward ready for anything and he lunged at me and narrowly missed. We turned in crouched positions in a circle and just then, I heard two bottles breaking behind me.

Gangster and Mary were on each side of me yelling at the guy in Spanish that they were going to cut his balls off. He turned and ran and I was relieved as the two girls turned and laughed at the whole incident. I even went so far as to get a group of hookers together and I told them the truth. They were beautiful people, so I lifted them up and told them so.

"Get a new dress and some makeup and I'll take you to where you don't have to turn ten tricks a night to get a fix and have enough for a *wakeup*. All you'll have to turn, is one."

This caught their ear and off we went to boost dresses and makeup and all the things a lady needs.

I took them to a club, a club where heroin dealers frequent and got them a date for the night. It worked, they got all the drugs they wanted and so did I. All the tricks that were turned in one evening were only one. It was a change for them and a change for the better, but it was like the lesser of two evils. I must say, I really empathized for these women and what they had to put up with to make it through the drug scene, but most of all I admire their courage and strength. I lost touch with the girls after I got busted and was out over the weekend.

I lost my job again being late to work or not showing up at all. I made the call in, but I was released for not being at work. I filled an appeal with the Employment Office, but by the time, I won and I could get money, I was busted again.

I had been frequenting an abandoned building where other homeless people and myself holed up to fix and get a good nights sleep. We often shared our drugs if for some reason someone was short, because we knew the next time we might be short. Some people who came there were not so good at sharing and just wanted to take.

While I was waiting for the outcome from the Employment Office, I was selling all that I had left from my jewelry business. I sold anything, even tools. Word got around that I had gold and silver to sell and that I carried it in my car. I just didn't think anyone would try to rip me off for it and it wasn't much.

One evening while I had just gotten in from a score and in a hurry to fix, another guy came in and wanted me to give him my heroin for some coke. I saw him earlier at a dealer's house and gave him a ride to a gas station next to another dealer's house and now he was back. I don't like coke and I told him, "no, get the f__k away." He didn't like that and pulled a knife on me. I told him, "put the knife away or I am going to shove it up your ass."

Now if you're a dope fiend and your high gets threatened, it really pisses you off. This guy just thought he was king of the hill or something because you can tell he was already high. He wanted my dope and my keys and I told him, "no way man."

As he got closer to me, I told him to "back-off" and "you don't want to do this." I was looking for something to grab so I could hit him with it, but it was too dark in there. I spilled the dope out of my spoon and almost fell over a bunch of trash and debris when he lunged. I caught the tip of the knife in my knee, got balanced and hit him hard to the ribs. I picked up a piece of metal and began to beat him with it. I was in a rage and I was merciless at this maniac, who just spilled my dope and tried to kill me.

I heard him fall to the ground and for a moment I took all the rage I had been experiencing out on this guy. He picked the wrong set of circumstances and the wrong frame of mind to get stupid. I knew I hurt him bad, because I could hear gurgling from his chest. I got scared and tried to salvage what dope I had left and fix the remains. I left the scene in a hurry, figuring the other guys would find him there and take care of him. After all, he was their friend, not mine.

I couldn't sleep that night, "what if he's dead," I thought. "Maybe I should go back?" or "Maybe I should call the cops." I was restless and the next day, I found out that he had died and I was now really scared. Word got out in the street that the cops were looking for anyone who hung out there for questioning. I wouldn't go back there, because I knew someone there had mentioned my name and I was too scared to turn myself in.

I was feeling rotten and guilty, like defiled really badly. Word got out that he was really a bad guy and had been threatening his connection and robbing people at knifepoint in the area. It was said that even his connection had put a contract out on him. It was an excellent opportunity to get some dope, so I told his connection that I was the one who killed him. That was a *scam* that was a mistake, because his connection had me arrested. Great, now they're going to think, I'm some kind of hit man and I'm not. This was getting very serious and when I did get arrested, the police thanked me, because they wanted this guy bad and that I did them a favor. Now, I sit in this cell wondering what life has in store for me and even what does the afterlife have. How am I going to explain to God, that I took one of his children in anger, in rage even though he tried to kill me.

After some intense moments during court proceedings my attorney told me that he made a deal and to cop a plea. Although I was remorseful, I still felt that I didn't do anything wrong.

"Your only hope is to plea bargain for a lesser charge," he said.

The State Attorney Generals Office took over the case and made me an offer, "Six years for voluntary manslaughter".

At the time voluntary manslaughter carried, three, six, and eleven years. I was working part time in a jewelry store and my boss had guns. He told me, "if anyone looked suspicious to keep a gun on them from under the counter" when he buzzed them in. "Shoot right through the counter if necessary or until I say, it's ok". Had it happened there, I would have been fine. They said it was because it happened at the *shooting gallery*.

I told my attorney to go back and try for the three years and that I didn't deserve the six years. I was willing to do the three, just behind the fact of the way I was feeling and the remorse I had. They did not agree and told me the six years was final. I took it and was soon on a bus to

Chino Hills on my wife's birthday and turned over to the California State Department of Corrections.

"Chino"
(Analogy of Hope)

◆

Chino is the Intake Reception Center for Southern California and it's called the Guidance Center. There, prisoners are evaluated for various reasons including psychiatric stability, the intensity of their offense, and risk factors like if they have AIDS or are a *snitch* in need of protective custody. Another factor is that if someone is a repeat offender or habitual criminal and belongs to any gangs.

I was housed overnight and in the morning sent to the West Yard. It is a layover area where the approximate stay is one month until your evaluation is processed and you find out where you're going to be sent. While I waited, I met a couple of people, one from Santa Barbara and the other from Cochilla Valley. They were both young and have never been in prison before so I kind of took them under my wing so to speak. I kept trying to find the answer to why I was here and the purpose for it. I mean, I know what I did, but I figured maybe that the lord wanted me to help those in need when they crossed my path. So I had two here, right now, so why not. I didn't know I was about to end up in a roll of father, mother, doctor, lawyer, preacher, brother, counselor, and friend.

One evening we went to church service and it was an "all welcome" kind of thing and I'm not particular to jumping up and down. I know the Holy Ghost thing and this was more Baptist orientated, but I was kind of drawn there. I wasn't sure why I was drawn there, maybe because it was the holidays and I missed my family. Maybe because I felt I'd find an answer there or find some peace of mind.

In the service and during the prayer session to cast out demons a guy near the back of us suddenly started to shake and make noises. Now I've seen people speaking in tongues, but never this intense. He was speaking a different language, yelling and cursing something. I interpreted it to a person stomping and yelling at a demon to get out of his house. At the same instant, I pictured an African native coming out of his hut, stomping at chickens to get out of his yard. The chickens were the demons and it sent chills running through me and knew this was not a fake, it was actually happening, but in a different time.

After the service, I knew that I had to help. I had kept it in my mind that this kind of stuff is all a fake, then this was laid out before me. I had my answer, whoever god throws before me; I'll help as best I can and with whatever knowledge I obtained until now. Helping people without expecting anything back, unconditional and even in a more type of penance being self fulfilling. After all, this must be what he wants because I should have been dead long ago. I also knew that I had to remain honest with myself and that I had to take a lot of lumps. Stuff that I wouldn't put up with before. I just had to do it no matter what.

I also knew that I had a lot of time to change my life and it wasn't going to be easy. It took about fifteen years learning how to survive the drug scene, jails and institutions. It would take that long to make it back to being a *normie* if ever there is such a state. I'd have to find out why I am still alive and what it is exactly I'm supposed to do. It had to get better because how much lower could I go than this. After a few weeks of convict socializing in the yard, playing handball, cards and finding out the latest news, who's busted, dead, and stories both inside and out, I got my *ducat* to catch the *Grey Goose*.

It was time for the shackles again and I caught a bus to Soledad State Prison. The two guys from Cochilla and Santa Barbara were also on the bus and I felt better to have some familiar faces around. We stopped at the medical facility CMF near Santa Barbara to drop off some inmates, then on to Soledad in the City of Martinez in Central California. All I heard about that place is that there was a lot of lock downs from fights and stabbing and it's always under the gun.

When we got there, We were separated, searched and placed in a holding cell type of warehouse. It was clean and spotless and cages contained many television sets that have been confiscated for one reason or another. Later I found out that the number issued televisions were for specific inmates only. They were lost during a card game, betting, and drug trades, taken away or given away. When found and the number does not match the inmate, it is confiscated. "This place is going to be a whole world of it's own", I thought.

We filled out some forms, got a box lunch and were sent to X-wing. This is a reception center for about ten days if you don't get into any trouble and is under heavy security. It was the first time I saw so many guns, "m-sixteen's" the guards carried, and will shoot you if you got out of line.

I landed in a cell with a young man from Norwalk, who was in for killing two people in a drive by shooting. "What a shame", I thought, he just turned eighteen and was sixteen when it happened, but was tried as an adult. When you land in a cell with someone you don't know, it's a curiosity to see what they are about, so a certain line of questioning and observance is helpful. After all, you don't want to wake up to some psycho homosexual predator trying to rape and choke you. Not to imply that all homosexuals are predators, but in the prison system more likely to encounter them. No, you try to figure if you can take this guy if it becomes necessary. Luckily, this kid was easy to get along with, had a sense of humor and was very street wise for his age. He was probably sizing me up too and for the next ten days we spent a lot of time together talking.

We got to take a shower every other day upon request. The only things we were allowed to take out of the cell were shower shoes, shorts, soap and towel. We backed up to the tray slot in the door to get hand-cuffed, then let out to get shackled around waist and ankles. On the cat-walk above were guards with rifles watching every move we made. We were led to the shower area cell and the electric door slid closed behind us. We backed up to the bars and the handcuffs and shackles were removed, then allowed into the shower area through another gate. Next to the gated shower area is a guard sitting in a chair in a cage, watching, and a rifle lay across his knee. This is the highest level security for new arrivals. As I looked around at this new life, I just let out a sigh and knew it just had to get better.

I knew that time would change things and I just had to stay out of trouble. I would try and navigate this situation without incident, but also knew that sometimes avoiding trouble is very difficult.

As the days passed and I learned more of my new found friend here, I explained to him the difficulties ahead. He had more of a tough guy approach and wouldn't admit being scared.

"That's fine" I told him, "but it can lead to trouble, because there is always some other guy trying to pull you down."

He was a fighter too and I told him how to use it to his advantage and not for foolishness. As I found out, he was more worried about keeping an image and I told him about false pride, to be very careful.

I wasn't sure if I was getting through to this tough kid, but on Christmas Eve, I guess he let his guard down and made me a Christmas card out of what little things we had. I'll always remember this kid because he seemed to understand the seriousness of life and that we are not special. There are many people out there with more serious prob-lems than ours and who have been through a lot tougher times. He also called me "bedrock twist" and I liked that name. For me, the bedrock is a foundation and the twist, is the turn around in my life. The kid gave me hope without realizing it and I got the feeling that I got through to him. I still can't believe it, but I actually left that cell happy.

After the ten days, I was transferred to what was called "G-Wing". On the way there was many paintings on the walls—positive and cultural stuff. The inmates walked close to the walls and stayed out of the center of the hallway. I did the same and passed many doors and looked in every time I got the chance. You don't want someone thinking your *mad dogging* them. We past the *SHU unit* where I was told Manson and Serhan were. Great! "Why do I got be in the same place with these guys", I thought.

When we got to G-Wing, we were told that it was in lock down status from fighting just days before. Inmates got shot from ricocheting bullets and a guard was hit. As I looked around, it was all cement, steel doors, rails, and bars. On each end of the wing were two landings that led upstairs and at the very top close to the roof were guards with guns, watching any movement.

I was assigned a cell near the entrance of the building. I was to stay here for a *minute*. My new cellmate was also from Norwalk, in for an armed robbery and doing eleven years. I was amazed at the books he had, it was like a library inside, but mostly bibles. That was ok with me, I was just hungry for any literature I could get my hands on and reading I did, day and night. Books were very scarce in this section of the prison, why, I don't know. Maybe it was a sign of weakness, but I didn't care, I knew myself. I was grateful to have books. No sooner was this new-found treasure, when word was going from cell to cell, "the shuttle blew up and they're all dead". There was no radio or television in this cell and it took three days before I could find out any more information on what happened with the space shuttle, "Challenger".

We did get out for two days and go on the yard for a walk, but fights broke out and we were locked down again. While inside my cell one evening, I was reading about the apostles, Peter and Paul, how Jesus gave Peter the keys to the Kingdom and when Peter was put in prison by the Romans and also locked in a cell.

Exactly when I was reading the part when the prison began to shake and his shackles broke loose, the building began to shake and sway back and forth. I thought I could see the steel door bend sideways as the building shook. I could hear yells to open up, and the fear in the tone of the voices. I took it as a message and I must be on the right track, because to me, this was loud and clear. I looked at my cellmate and could see in his eyes that he agreed this was a powerful message. It was very interesting, because just as soon as I started to think about how scary it was to be locked in with the building crumbling around, unable to get out or starve to death, it took away the message and fear began to creep in. Not funny ha ha, but funny weird how the grace of God can comfort one in need. I didn't care if I died or not, I just knew something was coming for me and that it would be good. I mean, it's impossible to go through all the things that I have done and still be alive.

*   *   *

After the lockdown, I met up with my two friends, the ones from Santa Barbara and Cochilla, and we got to walk the yard. We stuck together until we got the feel of the place. Like I said before, there are two different factors of Mexicans if you are gang related, one from the North and one from the South. The guys from the North wear red as a favorite color and Southern Cal wear blue as a favorite color. We really didn't care about colors, just the fact that we had to know who was who and stay away.

On one afternoon while walking the track, two guys wearing red running shorts followed us. If we stopped, they stopped and they matched our speed or slowed down as we did. My friends were getting nervous and frankly, so was I. I think it was a game of nerves and I was getting tired of it, so I told my friends to cut across the infield.

Knowing the inmates bury their shanks in the field and in the weight pile, I told them that at one point stop, turn around and look at them casually, while I stayed behind them digging in the ground like I was digging up a shank.

As soon as we did this maneuver, the two Northern guys stopped, started talking to each other, and as I stood up with my hand cuffed and looked at them, they got the message and left. It was a bluff, but it worked and we felt better. My friends kept telling me, "how did you know how to do that", and "I'm sure glad we met up".

I just told them "Experience and keeping a watchful eye, keeping your mouth shut helps. Besides, they may be back and really have knives", I said.

"Take a look around, it's not a game", I added.

As the days grew, we became more accustomed to how things worked, but then there are the days when the unexpected happens. I was playing handball with some homeboys from Orange County when I hit the ball and it flew over the backstop. So what? I had to go get it and it landed into a group of about twelve blacks. As I ran to get it, I saw where it went and as I ran, my brain was on alert and this could be trouble.

I told one of the black guys, "you got the ball?"

"Ball, I ain't seen no ball", he said,

"You see a ball?" he said to one of the others.

"Oh Christ", I thought. I couldn't back down, and I spotted the ball in the hand of a guy that had his shirt off with lots of tattoos.

"And what's that there in your hand?" I said.

"I found this ball," he said.

"Okay", I muttered with a smile and without really much thought, I made a motion back to the handball court calling the guys over. I knew no one was looking, but these guys didn't know that. Finally, after a few tense moments that seemed like hours the silence was broken.

"Man! Why don't you give this guy the ball, before you start some shit!" the short guy said.

The shirtless guy tossed me the ball.

"Thank you, thank you very much" I added.

As I jogged back to the courts with much relief and a big smirk on my face, I thought, Mario, only you can get yourself into something like this. Actually, I thought I was pretty diplomatic about the whole thing.

When I got back to the court, the people I was playing with were mad because I had been gone so long.

"Yeah, thanks for the support", I said in a disgusted tone.

They didn't even see what was happening. I was beginning to notice that this place had a reputation for being tough, but so far it was mild, stupid things and a game of nerves more than anything else. I talked to some friends about it and they confirmed my thoughts telling me that this is why they call it "Silly-dad". It was ironic and maybe for the best.

I was attending church regularly and I had the opportunity to talk to the parish priest. I told him that I would like to make my first communion and how I was unable because my baptismal papers were lost. He confirmed that although we can't be baptized twice, he would take the initiative and baptize me again anyway. I was elated at the thought, but all I wanted was to be confirmed of my first communion. He gave me an adult catechism book to read completely and told me to write to the churches in the area where I was baptized. I wrote to the churches for records to no avail. The church where I was originally baptized was indeed burned down and the records lost, so I wrote to the surrounding churches for any information they could provide.

After much preparation and searching, my childhood dream was about to become true. As always and true to form of my life, something got in the way. I got transferred to the North Yard the day before the baptism was to take place. I felt let down, like a storm was brewing over my head, and I tried not to let the confusion set in. Why? I kept asking, as if I was going to get an answer. I had forgiven the church for what it did to me as a child and perhaps it just wasn't the time for me. Maybe there will never be a time for me.

A Correctional Officer walked me over early in the morning; it was drizzling and cold. Everything was wet, damp with the air of despair. I remembered as a child that whenever it rained I would get into trouble, like the day Tommy I and ran away.

I carried all I could and the guard told me, "you're better off getting rid of some of that stuff". He was right, all I had was a bunch of junk I collected, but it was my junk never the less and some had sentiment. I also had a lot of street clothes, like Levi's, socks and tennis shoes.

Looking at the place on the walk in, it looked cleaner, but smaller also, at least the yard was smaller. The inmates had an air of suspicion, if they stared I stared back until they looked away first. Some looked paranoid, like they would give you a double take out of the corner of their eye. Others would talk loud enough for you to hear and they were wondering where I was from, North or South is all they cared. This bunch actually looked meaner than the last bunch I just came through. They looked more seasoned and you could tell they had a settled routine in place. That was good because the meaner you look, the more respect you get. Prison values are so different than for the outside. It's up to you, if you lose your respect then you'll be an outcast or in some cases cast out. I went in with a poker face, all the time in search mode for a familiar face, anyone I previously knew would bring the tension down a bit. People don't realize that when you hit the state system, you better have made a few friends and not have crossed any barriers in some barrio war less you better beware of your back. You can feel it, the tension permeates your body to be on guard.

Inside and in less than a minute, I saw a friend called Mark, a young white kid I previously met in Sierra and had taught him to read and try to stay out of trouble. Seeing him there, with a Cheshire cat smile on his face, and knowing he didn't make it on the outside from the last time we met and neither did I.

He just yelled out, "I'll catch you later when you come back homes".

Now everyone on the tier knew I was from the South and wouldn't you know it, I was assigned a cell with a Norteno. I couldn't have cared less, but I didn't want to send the wrong message and I wasn't in a gang so on the second tier, I went in. He had his routine all set and was very clean. Frankly, I was glad cause I never got to talk to a Norteno before, so this was going to be a test and a test in front of everyone's eyes. As it turned out, he wasn't any different than I. He had a little pressure from his peers, but no threats and it was just talk. He wasn't in a gang either and at least he was honest because he liked doing drugs and this system wasn't about to stop him. He offered, but I said no. I must've been crazy, I actually said no.

I was changing slow, but changing. It was the same thing when I got out in the yard, lots of looks, but I soon found some people I knew from doing time in one jail or another. All they could suggest was for me to watch my back, and that it gets crazy in here from time to time. I could deal with that.

I wasn't in the cell a week when I was called downstairs to see a counselor. I couldn't imagine what it was for, maybe I was getting transferred again. No, when I arrived at the counselor's, she informed me that she had some bad news. My family flashed before me and I was right. My mother had called the institution and informed them that my grandfather Martin had passed away. She also informed them that we were very close and they should keep an eye on me. I resented that and told them I would be ok and could I please go back to my cell. She also told me that arrangements could be made for me to go to the funeral. I heard about these arrangements and I didn't want my family to see me in chains. My throat began to swell up and I swallowed back the tears.

As I walked back I couldn't show any weakness and kept my head up and walked straight. I told my cellmate what had happened and I think he was shocked at how open I was. I remember telling him that openness would give me strength. No matter how weak it may have looked, in it was strength and he respected that.

I sat quiet in my upper bunk, popped open a soda and quietly cried at the memories while starring out of the barred windows. How I would go with him on the truck from barrio to barrio and how I would go over during his last days and give him a shave.

"*Grampa*, how do you want your moustache?" I said,

"*Como Charlie Chap*" he would say.

Charlie Chaplin was his favorite silent movie star.

Most of my homeboys from Orange County were in another wing next door and kept telling me to move next door. I put in a request to move not knowing that the friction next door was notorious and my request was granted within a day.

I was celled up with Flaco from Imperial Valley and he ran with the homies from Orange County. It was cool and I had to learn the ropes all the time keeping up an image of strength and integrity. All I had was my word and I meant to keep it.

I also had two relative brothers in the same wing. They were actually my brother-in-laws brothers and were both doing twelve years and working in the garment industry.

There was tension on the yard, but we all, or at least I did, felt comfortable enough with the numbers we had so no one would mess with us. After all, one of us was a fool homosexual, and if you got a cell with this guy, you better be ready for a fight to last until the next unlock cause this guy was relentless. That was his preference and we called him "*mudpacker*". He would just laugh, but give you a look like, wait till me and you are together alone. I wasn't afraid because I knew I could take him. He had a glass jaw, but not everyone knew that. Deep inside, I hated him for what he is; a sexual predator, but I smiled and remained friendly.

The other guys were from Anaheim, Stanton, Delhi, and Santa Nita. It was a good group and we passed the time comfortably, but this had a price. Had I known to keep my eyes and ears more open, what happened next should have never happened.

*　　　　　*　　　　　*

Flaco and I were released at breakfast and we exited our cell as usual.
Flaco noticed that there were only whites and blacks going to breakfast
and just a few of the Mexican population.

"Watch your back", he said as a warning, "Something's going down".

We saw others we knew and asked,

"What's up"?

No one knew or couldn't tell, but we were wary and ready for anything.

Breakfast went off without a hitch, but you could feel the tension in
the air and the vibes *mad dogging* coming from the blacks was very bad.
I told Flaco,

"I think something already went down".

"Your right, he said.

We found out that a black dude got *hit* just before chow. We also
found out that it was Mexicans, who did it.

"*Ponte trucha*" he said.

We walked back to the wing, watching that no one got too close and
entered the cell enclosure area. We were on the bottom tier and
remained in front of our door with our backs to it, watching the pro-
gression of the black insults across the way. They seemed to be yelling
and cursing at someone on the third tier above them. As I watched, I
saw one black guy breaking a mop handle to use as a weapon across the
way from me. The others were gathering broom handles and metal
dustpans and who knows what else they had.

I wasn't about to become a casualty, and I didn't have a weapon. I
stepped up to the table in front of my cell, put my hand in my pocket
making it look like I had a shank in it, and put my foot up on one of the
table seats. I looked above me and it looked safe enough to know no one
was going to drop anything on my head. The blacks across the way were
yelling remarks and making taunting gestures and communicating with
other blacks on the second and third tiers. Most of the activity was happening across from us. I began to focus on them, not wanting to take my
eyes off of them, standing casual and looking mean. Every now and then,

I would give them a gesture, still with my hand in my pocket, like come on then, I'm right here, and want some of this, come and get it then.

It was my imagination, but I thought, they thought I was crazy. A few blacks ran to the rear landing and went up the stairs to the third tier. That's when all hell broke loose, as the fighting began up there on the third tier. People were actually jumping off the tiers, trying to get away and it got very bloody. I felt the tension melt away from me and said to myself, "Thank God".

When I finally turned around, I was in shock, because I was alone and there was no one behind me backing me up. No wonder the blacks thought I was crazy. I thought I had all these people behind me and they were at the entrance gating about ten yards to my left yelling for the guard to let them out. I was so disappointed, all these tough guys crying for help, trying to get out of harms way.

I suddenly realized the bells were going off and you could suddenly hear the goon squad coming with jingling keys and equipment. A warning shot was fired at a bucket of sand and everyone knew the next one would be somebody. I backed up to my cell door, got down on the ground and waited. I looked for Flaco and to this day, I still don't know where he went. "No wonder they call this place Sillydad", I thought. We were locked down while an investigation went underway.

I sat in my cell and sounded Flaco about his leaving and not saying anything, he was two doors down, but I wasn't buying it. I was mad at the situation and mad because we were not forewarned of the incident. They should have let us know because it involves all of us. They acted on their own accord and even though we were not a gang, it would have helped to know.

As I lay in my bunk, thinking about the whole situation, somehow I knew this was the last time I'd ever go to prison again. I saw it was different than I'd imagined and this incident and the way prisoners act was stupid. How easy it was for one person to put the life of another in jeopardy over some foolishness. We were fed in the cell and about four days later it was my turn to see the inquiry board. Everyone in the wing had to go and when I got there, it was more like a security hearing. The lieutenant in charge asked me if I saw what happened and I said, "no", and that was it.

Then he recognized me from Sierra,

"Aren't you an ex-camper?" he said.

"Yes" I said.

"Do you want to go back to camp?"

"Sure", I said with a smile.

That was it, I was on the next bus back to Sierra and my security level was lowered a step. I was totally surprised and glad to be leaving this place. It wasn't what I expected and I suspect, it could've been worse. I felt sorry for those who had to do time there, and they only learned how to instill fear. There were a lot of idiots inside who seamed to want to cause trouble. The racial intensity was immense. If you could feel it you would know what I mean. When you hit the streets, it's like it never happened. Whites, black and brown do the same things and almost never have problems like in here. Racial comments are different and feelings set aside, but once in prison, it changes and reverts to survival of the fittest and fight or flight syndrome is at least ten times greater than outside. This is just my opinion.

"Sierra Conservation Center"
(The Road Home)

◆

It was early spring when I arrived at Sierra. It was still cold and raining at the base of the Sierra Mountains where the base camp is located near a town called Jamestown. Jamestown has a gold rush era history and still looks to this day like the cowboy, miner, preacher and saloon town of old pioneer days. Many of the buildings look just like the old forty-niner days. After all, this is the mother load country, which gets many tourists each year.

At the gates of Sierra, I could immediately see that things had changed since I last was here. There were so many inmates in both yards, more than I ever saw before. I could tell it was overcrowded as the inmates from both entry gates watched to see who the new arrivals were. They waited in expectation to hear news from other institutions or news from home or just to see how many of each ethnicity came in.

The base camp has two yards, the "*Mariposa*" and "*Calaveras*" yards and I went to the Mariposa yard. It had a higher level of security and an added gun tower of which I quickly took notice. We were taken to an area where we were searched and our personal items were either confiscated or sent home unless they were approved. I brought my legal heating element to make coffee from Soledad and it passed inspection. Such a little thing meant so much when it's all you got.

127

When I entered the dorm area, it was a surprise to see that the usual eighteen-man dorm was now a thirty-six-man dorm with bunk beds. That also meant thirty-six men to two showers and two toilets. At least there were no bars on the windows, but the windows were horizontal five-inch by three foot slats that opened like a louver. During the day the dorms were unlocked hourly to let those going to and from work, access. The whole place had twice as many people and was badly over-crowded. I knew this was going to be a challenge because overcrowding created tensions that only those who lived it knew what it was like. It's like driving on the freeway and being constantly cut off, tailgated with constant delays, flaring up tempers and holding it in until....well, we all have heard of road rage and this is like that! It happens.

I found out I had to spend two years there before my security would be lowered to minimum and that was only if I stayed out of trouble. Only then, could I go back to a satellite camp and with minimum security.

I knew I had to find a job soon as I constantly told myself that I was not going to waste this time and I was going to get something out of being here. I wanted to learn something positive and new and why not I was here and there were resources available so I took advantage of them.

I started at the library where I taught myself how to type every chance I got when the typewriters were available. It was first come first serve plus other inmates were willing to help out with hints at typewriting. This camp had many blue-collar criminals with an education beyond high school and all were willing to lend a hand. I made ends meet by reading and writing letters for inmates who could not read or write. Letter writing was very interesting and personal. That's how I became so close to some inmates who really didn't know how to communicate from a gut level that was sincere, warm, and loving. Someone on the exterior could seem mean and nasty, but really how one feels, I found, is hard to get out. Once the experience is successful then you see a change. I believe I changed many lives or at least touched them to see another way. I was offered payment in sodas, cigarettes, soup, coffee, or anything that had value and could be used to make time easier. Some inmates gave me more than I thought the help was worth and I gave them stuff back because they gave more than they could afford. I also wrote to the courts on appeals for time served and when an inmate got at least six months off of their sentence, I was rewarded handsomely.

At the same time, I was trying to get a job working for the training center as a yard coordinator. The training center was a joint program with the, California Department of Corrections and California Department of Forestry to train inmates on fire line safety and physical fitness training. A friend from the family in Norwalk had the position and was soon to be released. After his release I got the job which paid about one-dollar-thirty-cents a day. I worked in the gym, which wasn't a gym anymore. With all the overcrowding, the gym was being used fore new arrival holding area and it was a base camp. The inmates in base camp status had much more privileges than the rest. It seemed ironic because these guys were fenced off from the rest, inside the gym and it was loud all the time. The job was enough to buy my coffee and cigarettes, plus I was able to send home a little to my wife and I had enough to bargain with or give away as I chose.

This job was clerical and I had a gym clearance and access to both yards. I knew I would be an asset, plus the coach had a new electric typewriter, which I couldn't wait to get my hands on. It also had benefits because not only did I help the coach train the new recruits for fire fighting training, but I also coordinated all the yard activities including, table games like cards, dominoes, chess, checkers, I also set up soccer games, league basketball. I set up card tournaments and helped set up the bingo games. I kept both yards busy to distract inmates from violence and I was proud of what I did.

I also submitted a proposal to the State of California for justification to have videos connected to the dorms. It passed and the coach rented videos of recent releases. This was a hit with the inmates and the requests for movies came flooding in. I put out a list to choose from and a popular vote was taken with the final say of the coach, nothing X-rated. Later I proposed to have satellite dishes placed out in the camps and it was passed. There were previous proposals done for the same things, but it sure did feel good to be heard and lift my self-esteem when I actually saw the changes being made. I was in the right place at the right time and I can say that because I was on a mission to make better anything that came my way. And I did.

In between all my newfound activities, I was able to play music with other inmates who were previously in bands and even one that was famous. The last time I saw him was at a three day festival called "Newport 69" held in "Devonshire Downs" where all the great bands came to play and he played with Jimi Hendricks.

The church had a room set aside that we could use and it included equipment. I played the drums along with a bass player, rhythm and lead guitarist. I also played the harmonica when I didn't play drums. We, as a group, were very fortunate to have this ability and thankful for the facilities.

I also wrote poetry and actually got published in a compilation of prison poetry. I dreamed of using a computer, but none were available in this setting.

Once a month on Thursday nights I would help the coach with bingo and one time I asked if I could play also and he said it was ok. The prizes were game cards, cartons of cigarettes, baseball caps, chess sets.

On this particular night I kept winning and every time I won the coach would give me a dirty look. I must have won three cartons of cigarettes, three baseball caps and various decks of cards. He put a stop to my playing and was really angry. He thought I was cheating and I wasn't, it was just a lucky night for me. He couldn't see that and I forgot where I was. Even if it was a lower security prison, I was still a convict. He even went so far as to tell me, "Morales, before you leave this place, I want to know how you did it". He thought I had rigged the game somehow and wanted to know how I could get over on him. I told him the truth, I was lucky, but he couldn't accept that. So Coach Lopez, if you ever read this, it's the truth, get over it.

I learned how to draw portraits in color pencil. These are actually reproductions of portraits but come out excellent. Especially if you have that one particular beat up photograph, you have cherished for so long to come alive again.

Out in the yard, people looked up to me, I was a mediator and settled disputes. I couldn't walk the yard without someone calling me over to settle a dispute just because I worked for the coach. I volunteered to referee the soccer games. I don't know where I read it or if someone said it, but "we become what we do". Everything that I did here was positive and at the same time I tried very hard to improve myself in all aspects of life. I did a lot for the inmates here and in doing so, I did it for myself, too.

There was this one old man I knew of from my yard who really needed dental work. I don't think he had any family on the *outs,* so I arranged for him to be seen early. I also needed dental work to get my two front teeth fixed.

I lost my front teeth showing off, popping wheely's on my new Schwinn bicycle at age ten. When the front tire was in the air and I was trying to make it the length of six houses, the front tire fell off. Needless to say, the front forks went down right into the asphalt and so did my face. I lost both front teeth, which were my second set and I looked like a pirate without them.

The old man and I got into the Dentist office, but the clerk wanted a *kick down* in order to be moved up in line and there was a six- month wait. Well, I got angry and told him I was going to take care of him, but not in the way he thought. He thought he was safe because he was on the Calaveras yard and didn't know I had access to both yards.

I approached him and told him, "what do you mean charging people for better service".

He said, "man, this is my hustle, I got to make something on the side".

"Yea, but not at the expense of everyone else and especially those who need help and can't afford it. I got a notion to take you down right here" I said.

He was looking scared now and should be.

I told him, "look, you abuse a privilege and that ain't right, I'll kick you down something, but it ain't because I have it to give, you got to think of those who can't and give them a break, you hear what I'm saying"?

I heard about this dude from some of my friends and knew this would happen one day. As it turned out, I got a new flipper for my front teeth and I could smile without covering my mouth. The old man got a brand new set of *chompers* and didn't look so old after they were in.

One of my favorite memories of this place may seem odd to you, but it is the water. I'll never forget the water. We were so close to the Sierra foothills that the water was so sweet when you drank from the faucet it tasted like soda water without the fizz and my church friends called it, "Adams Ale". When you took a shower, the soap and shampoo would lather immensely and seemed to last forever. The cleansing effect, even without the soap was almost spiritual. The coffee made with this water was beyond description and it tasted so good.

I also liked to run almost everyday, rain or shine I ran six miles, twenty-four laps around the track. I remember my compulsiveness because one hot, humid July afternoon, no one was outside from the heat and I was running the track, alone in my own world at peace. Suddenly it started to rain, big, giant drops of water like a sign from heaven, cooling my hot aching body and I gave thanks. It seemed like I had the whole place to myself and I was on top of the world and truly blessed.

My clerical skills advanced to a professional level after a year on this yard and it was getting time to go again.

It wasn't all easy going though, because there were many clothing and food shortages and fights broke out and we got locked down. One inmate even died, but for what, because we didn't have the basic necessities like clean clothes, fresh bedsheets. If you were fortunate enough to have new prison issue clothes, you washed them yourself, because if you turned them in, you would get back only raggedy looking clothes.

Just because we are inmates in prison doesn't mean we don't have any self-respect. Most of the inmates here couldn't read or write and had a tough time of it growing up, so had to be tough and aggressive. It could be worse, but intensify envy and covetousness and the only thing that will come of it is violence. The administration knew that, but said their hands were tied.

After the 12 months, it was time to leave this place and move on to better things. My security was lowered to minimum and I was transferred next door on the Calaveras yard. It was like starting all over again and since this yard was the area for transfers and training graduates and the security was lower, the clothing issue was better. The privileges were also better and we could interact with news coming from one camp to another. Who was there? Which one is better? How the food was?

I had to find a new job and I wanted to go to camp as an "in-camp clerk". I kept my ears open and asked around about clerical jobs. I soon found all the information I needed. I found the camp lieutenant in charge of the camp positions for work and skills. He gave me a short test, I past easily, as it was just a few questions and some spelling.

It was just a short time before I was transferred to a camp in central California called, Camp Miramonte. Now I was working for the California Department of Forestry and making two dollars and fifteen cents a day. I was excited as I arrived because it was snowing and this was the second time in my life I had been in snow.

The camp was an older camp and looked like a Christmas scene from a post card with snow on the roofs of a very small town. Here and there, smoke came from a chimney, a few people walked about with tools in their hands in heavy coats and boots.

The Administration Office was prominent and set aside from the bungalows where the inmates were housed. I was quickly introduced to my new job details and although I didn't like the distance from home, it was great to be outdoors in the mountains. After an orientation about camp rules and what was expected of each of us, I was shown the rest of the camp work areas, kitchen, hobby areas, and common day rooms where we could watch television or play pool.

I unpacked my gear and waited for the crews to come just to see if I knew anyone. I didn't, I was too far north and far from home. I looked around the dorm at the different hobbies displayed on each crew members storage lockers. I noticed the type of wood, *Pepperwood*. I made a coffee table from Pepperwood at a previous camp. It gives off a smell that reminds me of fresh baked bread when it's *routered* or sanded.

There also was some work done with redwood, but I knew it didn't grow here, so it must have come from the camps farther north. I knew that during fire season, the crews would trade wood with other crews and these were very nice pieces. They made clocks that would hang or stand up, some with family pictures coated with a poured mixture of plastic that shined like glass. This camp had a very nice hobby program and it gave us time to learn work habits, sharing information and take pride in the work being done. We could also make a little extra money selling the pieces off to family and friends.

When the crews came in, they sized me up as I did them. It's always the same when someone new came, the big guy had to impress his dominance catharting on others just to prove he was boss man in the dorm. At least there was no disrespect to me, but I didn't like this guy and took note of him just in case he tried the same with me. I wouldn't let people like that get away with it.

I wasn't there two weeks and an opportunity came for me to go to a camp closer to home, it was called, Camp Bautista located near the town of Hemet. I was taken to a point somewhere in central California where we met up with another Suburban vehicle going South. We ended up in Chino at another camp where we waited to be picked up by our last destination transfer vehicle.

Chino, Now I had minimum security and it was great to be outside of the razor wire fences again, only this time I was a new person and ready to get on with my new life. As I looked over at the fences from Chino Central, I remembered the days of chains, razor wire and gun towers. I thanked God for the transition in my life where I was and where I was heading. I wanted to build distance from my past. I couldn't change the past, but the memory was still there, like a guardian protecting me from an unhealthy frame of mind.

There are a lot of guys inside doing time for stupid things, such as I did, lost without guidance. Some, suffering much worse than I ever did and had a much harder life than I did. So, why was it that I was still alive and getting away from it? I asked myself, feeling almost guilty for being on the way out.

The last leg of our trip took us through Riverside County to Hemet and on through to Bautista. That was fine with me because my brother lived just a few miles away and I could finally have some visitors. It had been over two years since I had visitors and I was looking forward to seeing my family again. I had been writing all along and they were supportive of my progress and of me.

This camp was new and when I saw the satellite dish, I was proud to see it and know that I had a part in it being there. The camp was nestled in a grove of oak trees next to a small creek. It looked bare and the dorms were actually trailers converted into housing for about 24 inmates each and there were four of them. One trailer was a shower area and even the Administrative Office, which were two trailers put together. This is a high desert area, hot during the day and cold at night. There is lots of low shrubbery around mostly Manzanilla brush, scrub oak and Yucca.

Again, I went through an orientation on camp policies, rules and regulations. I finally got my job as in-camp clerk and I quickly became involved in the camps operations for both the Corrections and Forestry Departments. I ordered supplies for the camp and maintained records.

I always did more than my share of work and both the inmates and the camp administration accepted me into the fold, so to speak. I also was the payroll clerk and kept record of all fire time hours. This camp had an excellent reputation for the quality of food and I was glad to be a part of that.

I now made fifty-six dollars per month, but my writing letter business fell off as the inmates had more family support and that was fine with me. I got involved in the orientation process for new arrivals and I led the AA and NA meetings to generate an interest on a weekly basis. This camp did wonders for my self-esteem and I pushed myself at self-improvement.

During the orientations I was given a part, actually I worked myself into it. I explained to the new arrivals that the camp had a particular interest in them and that the personnel were here to help. If anyone got into a position where they thought about running, to talk to me. There are ways to work things out if approached properly.

The camp remained tranquil and there were a few fights and one runaway while there, but it was minimal and expected. I began getting frequent visits from family and even had at times, three-day visits with my wife and daughter. My daughter was four years old now and I still remember her voice in my head yelling, "ta-ta open up". In my heart, I knew this was it and although the changes had been subtle, and slow, it never the less was happening. After all, it took 15 years to get into the drug scene so I couldn't expect to come out of it in a day or rush myself into a fast pace.

I did my work thoroughly and maintained an excellent rapport between the staff and inmates. It's a very difficult position for a clerk to work for the "man" and still be an inmate who sleeps in the same dorms. I got suspicious looks at times, but quelled it with an immediate confrontation. I had respect from both sides and I guess I could say I became quite the diplomat. I have many fond memories from this camp and after seventeen months, it was time to go out into the world again and prove myself to myself.

For the last seventeen months, I could hold my head up with pride and respect at having done an excellent job. I also knew that upon release that prestige would be taken away and I would be just another parolee convict. I had to hang on to what I had accomplished, believe in myself and trust in faith. I also got ready for release by making a resume while I still had a typewriter available. I tried to think of everything I could possibly need, including clothes, and the camp personnel allowed me to buy extra clothing. I had a positive outlook for the future, but reality had a funny way of dealing with us upon release.

I had gotten a driver's license the same day of my release and the two hundred dollars that the State gives you upon release. With that and three hundred extra dollars I had saved, I began a new life.

My very first stop upon arriving home, I visited my grandfather, who is now buried next to his beloved wife, my grandmother Maria.

When I got home and settled in from the welcome my family gave me, it was time for some reality checks. My wife had a run in with the parole officer that really upset me. They went into my home before I was released and treated my wife as if she were an inmate, going through everything in the apartment, removing all her good knives, telling her no weapons allowed in the home and that I could be a danger to her and my daughter. My wife was quite upset at the hostile approach of the parole officer.

As soon as I reported to the parole office, it was like back to day one after my arrest. Nothing in between counted and I had to fight so as not to fall into anger, an anger that eats at your soul like a cancer. I swallowed it down and I was determined to get over it and go on with my life.

       *   *   *

During my absence, thankfully the Social Services Agency gave my wife and daughter assistance. I had to apply for myself until I got a job. I remember the day I went in to the Welfare office to apply. The receptionist was very kind and I asked her questions about getting a job there as a clerk. She instructed me as to where to apply and I told her one day I would be working there also.

About one year later I was working there at the very same place. It wasn't easy, but I thank God for the family support that I had. Had it not been for that, it could have been worse or different.

I went to look for work daily and encountered many obstacles, like when I did get an interview, explaining why I made so little on my last job which was two dollars thirty-cents a day. I had to be honest because I didn't want to get fired six months down the line and that being dishonest is detrimental to my health. When I told the interviewer I was in prison, you could see their disposition change and this invisible wall come up between us. When that happened, I knew the interview was done. They were nice though and came up with all kinds of excuses, like my being overqualified for the position or they'd get in touch with me or the position may not be for me. I found myself thinking, maybe I'm too old and that it may be a factor on finding a job. I was 38 and to me that was getting old. I brushed it aside and kept looking.

In the mean time the parole office sent me to another service center, JTPA providing jobs, but it was for people with low reading skills and language barriers. They said, I was the first one to get a 100% on the test. I was in the wrong place and then they sent me to the EDD office to a special section for "hard to place" individuals. I felt like I had a handicap and I don't mean that in a derogatory way either. Even the smallest things seemed so big, like driving on the freeway. I kept at the fifty-five mile an hour speed limit, "your getting old" I thought, but people kept passing me, tailgating me. I was doing the posted speed, but it felt like I was getting in their way, moving back to the city where everyone is in such a hurry.

I wanted to do everything right, but somehow I was afraid. The only good feeling I got was when a police car pulled up behind me, I didn't have to worry because I was free and knew they weren't looking for me. Luckily these things passed and I did feel better later, then the speed limit was raised to sixty-five and it started all over again.

I also had to contend with building trust with my family because there were times when I would get a look like they didn't believe me. I couldn't blame them, but it was like trying to shake an old skin. I knew it would take time and I was grateful, especially for my dad who treated me like the prodigal son come home. For the fatted calf, he gave me his truck, for a small fee, so I could use it to get back on my feet.

In between looking for a job and clothes, which I bought second hand, I looked for extra money collecting cans in the local parks when I had time and on weekends. Living on six hundred dollars a month just doesn't make it and I was bound to succeed in making it better. People give you dirty looks when you're out there with wife and daughter looking into garbage cans as a means of support. It was degrading, but I didn't care about that, I had to do what I had to do. I just had to find a job and soon.

The good thing was that my wife applied for HUD assistance and got an apartment in Irvine, a nice area of the county where the kids could go to a school without worry and have a decent education without fear of violence, drugs or graffittied walls at every turn.

Some of the jobs I had applied for made me feel like I was being discriminated. I applied for a job with the County of Orange knowing that they would not discriminate against me and I was fully qualified. It took awhile and by November of 1988, I was hired. It took me two and a half months to get a job and I did encounter resistance from the county interviews because of my background. I went to so many interviews I was almost to a pointless point, that place where dangerous, envious thoughts seem to permeate the mind. Then I met the nicest lady named,

Bernice, who listened to my story and said, "that could have happened to anyone".

"That's what I've been trying to tell them", I said.

She hired me and I started in a clerical position as an office assistant and was proud of it. The position that was only temporary, working at their records department, but was I ever grateful. It was the best decision I ever made, because working for Social Services is very positive and rewarding and for me, therapeutic.

As I write this book, I had many ups and downs and it makes me happy to know that there is a way for people to come out of addictions or find themselves. I may not be rich or make much money, but I'm happy and I like myself. Happy is so important and someday, I'll buy a home, it may take awhile but I know I can do it. I have a seven-year-old son now that want's a dog and I have been working for thirteen years. Thirteen years is the longest time I have ever been in the streets since 1973. If it had not been for telling the truth and having the courage to be honest with myself, I probably would have been dead by now.

I have hopes of working with children and teens and adults that have unfortunately encountered the same traumatic experiences that I have. Working with them before their feelings are scarred and covered up. I only wish that the times were different and we could reach these children before they get into trouble, like educating them. At least we can help them after they get into trouble and make sure they don't make the same mistakes I did. My only setback is having a criminal record and hopefully one-day, I can get it expunged.

Many people will not hire and honest ex-con and this is just to let you know that there are some of us out there, many of us. Take the time to listen when you hear their story. It surprised me to find just how many people are in the same situation and are still hurting inside. Not only abused children, but also the parents of abused children sometimes shun the child in isolation apart from ever being close to the parent; especially fathers. These people need reassurance, just like I do. But it took almost forty years getting it out into the open for the healing to begin, like a small voice crying out in a cement wilderness.

Had I opened up while I was in the, Family Program in Norwalk, I would have saved myself the torment of a prison life of twelve years and living with the fact everyday that I had taken away a life. Fear stopped me from opening up. Fear can be my best friend and my worst enemy. Fear takes away focus, direction and the ability to remain calm. Although I didn't make it through the rehabilitation process, I did learn about myself and my innermost feelings and how to speak up. Instead of using fear as an adrenaline generating motor to overcome obstacles in the flight mode, I use it as an asset to overcome speech and confrontation in a diplomatic fight mode. This also could be called turning aggression into assertiveness.

Today is a new beginning as each day is a relief from the dregs of addiction and self inflicted loneliness I created. No matter how much distance I build, I still have days that try to pull me down. Faith, prayer, and the faces of my children are very important at this stage. Family is important, friends are important. After all of this, I still have much room to grow and learning is a major part of my life even if it's only a little at a time, like small steps, down the path of happiness.

I enjoy my newfound freedom, every day is a new beginning and I have hope. As I enter this new millennium, love, prosperity, and cheer are at the forefront of my life. During the past few years, people at work ask me repeatedly, "why are you so happy all the time?" I just tell them "if you lived my life, you would know".

This book is not meant to accuse individuals or circumstances. I made some very foolish, ignorant decisions in my life. Some of you may think I deserved what happened to me and some may empathize with my plight. I don't place any blame on family or society. I am doing this for myself and in turn to help others by baring my soul.

I would like to impress, should this happen to you, get help any way you can. Speak out and tell someone you trust someone you love, but tell someone. Now days, there are many open doors for assistance. Take it, use it, get help no matter how painful it may seem. The pain of experiencing these horrendous acts, along with low self-esteem and fears, play a large part in any inaction and a negative part in any decisions we bear. As one of humanities children, dealing with any one of these can make ones life decisions, take the path of least resistance.

Had it not been for the help of others encouraging me and pointing out my defects and my willingness to accept them and make necessary changes, I may not have written this book. Perhaps this book is what I have been searching for, a way to stop the world so it can take a look at what we do, a look into ourselves, through "The Glass Window".

Bravo for thee my friends, Bravo!

Thank You,

Mario Morales

About the Author

◆

Born and raised in Southern California, this is my journey in searching for self and putting a perspective in my life and how this amazing discovery turned out to be a key element in helping others. I asked myself, who am I? I found an interesting person I never knew.

Glossary

◆

Acid: LSD, a hallucinogenic.

Acting out: When one catches an attitude and acts out of place or gets violent.

Artesia: Named after a street, which was later, named Raitt. Also a barrio in central west Santa Ana.

Atole': a hot chocolate drink.

Aun aye esperanza: there is hope.

Aye te va: here you go or here it comes.

Barrio: A community of neighborhoods, mostly poor, consistent of Mexican migrant farmworkers and those who stayed to stabilize the culture as families grew.

Bench: The bench is a tool they use for disciplinary matters or other purposes.

Beaner: A derogatory remark. Meaning of persons of Mexican decent, whose staple diet of beans and rice were affordable.

Beanie: A black or blue watch cap.

Beef: problem, criminal case or conflict.

Bone-yard visit: three-day conjugal visit, but usually without children.

Braserro: To embrace by giving a hand. In the late fifties the U.S. and Mexican government created a labor program to help harvest crops due to a labor shortage. The name brassero was later used as a derogatory remark.

Bubble: the tower or command post that oversees all activity through a one way window.

Bucked back: When a chain saw reverses force towards the operator.

Bucking: cutting logs after a tree is felled.

Buenos Dias: a salutation meaning hello or good day!

Burro: meaning stubborn / also a small Donkey.

Café con leche: coffee with milk

Calaveras: Skeletons

Carom shot: Derived from the game of caroms, much like the game of pool, when the cue ball strikes another ball and sets off a strategic chain of events. This also works with behavior and character patterns. Example: "I want to talk to the person who constantly leaves the toilet seat up". Thus, you know it is a man. I could say, "it is you reading this book, and land the game on you. It doesn't always work that way, but I hope you get the idea.

Cellies: cellmates

Chingao: exclamation slang for "messed up" only stronger using "f" word.

Chompers: Dentures

Chow: A time to eat, breakfast, lunch, or dinner.

Chowhall: The mess hall like a cafeteria where people gather to eat

Chuppie: baby bottle nipple

CMF: California Medical Facility

Como Charlie Chap: grandfathers word for, "like Charlie Chaplin" of silent films.

Cop: score a bag of dope

Cottonmouth: that's when your mouth is very dry and/or you can't get any moisture into your mouth because of smoking marijuana.

Detoxing: detoxifying

Don: of the highest respect when said before your name as in Don Martin (pronounced marteen)

Dressing out: dressings out of jail issue clothing into street clothes normally warn.

Ducat: bus ticket

Dummied up: Not speaking, like a statue or dummy.

Dyads: when we would pair off and converse with one other person or also called one on one.

Eh: you

El Modena: A barrio East of the city of Orange *en especial:* on special or for special sale of product

Ese: A Mexican gangster greeting of mutual respect. Some persons of my generation take it as derogatory especially if from another race. Equal to the "N" word for blacks.

Frajos: cigarettes

Frisco's: Much like the baggy pants of today's youth. Heavy cotton canvases and usually black.

Gabacho: white or Caucasian.

Gardeners hook: a three-pronged hook with triangle spikes for digging and cultivating.

Grey Goose: The ugly grey bus.

Grampa: our word for grandfather.

Haircut: A disciplinary measure, being told to "stand there, your on a monad, this is a discipline", and they would yell at you from the top of their lungs about the behavior you just presented.

Hit: A killing, usually by stabbing, but could mean by any other means.

Homes: Persons from the same neighborhood or county. Also called *homie.*

I knew what time it was: phrase meaning, I am aware of what is happening or what's going on.

In the spoon: using drugs.

Joint: A marijuana cigarette.

"JTPA": Job Training Partnership Act.

Kick down: a payment, usually cigarettes.

Lightweight: meaning, I didn't have an extended arrest record.

Logan: A barrio towards the North East of Santa Ana.

LSD: A hallucinogenic.

Ludes: Slang for Quaalude's, a very potent barbiturate

Mad-dogging: A form of expression use to intimidate. Much like when siblings look at each other when angry.

Mama: mother

Mariposa: butterfly

Menudo: A delicacy made from beef tripe, hominy and chili in a soup.

Mescaline: A hallucinogenic of a natural source such as peyote.

Mexican circle: forms of the children's games "duck, duck, goose".

Minute: time is slow here and could mean anything from a week to months.

, *Mi vida loca:* My crazy life, loca neutered for male or female.

Mocoso: snot nosed kid or kid with a runny nose.

Monad: To be silent, no speaking or talking or gestures.

Mudpacker: a homosexual preference of a predator.

Muerte: a murder

Nina: godmother

Nino pendejo: stupid kid

Normie: normal person.

"Nortenos": Northerners.

Old school: Usually persons from the previous generation relating to everything from, dance, music, jails, drugs and actually old schools. A way of identifying with another.

Orale: hey, alright, hello

Out of it: drunk or on drugs.

Outs: outside the walls

Packing: smuggling dope into an institution.

Pan de semita: A Mexican Milk, but not too sweet, with a coating of flower, cinnamon, mixed with a small amount of sugar.

Pan dulce: Mexican sweet bread of a variety

Papa: father

Pendejo: dummy, soft meaning of stupid.

Pepperwood: California laurel, where the "bay leaves" used for cooking came from.

Perdoname: Pardon me, but not as in an "excuse me" in a grocery store, but more like asking for a pardon from a governor or priest.

Pigeon talk: A local slang language of the island like, "try smile, I promise no going broke your face".

Pocho: non-Spanish speaker who was born in the U.S.

"Ponte trucha": to be on guard or be careful.

Primo: cousin

Pruno: a homemade wine, favored, named and enjoyed by inmates. Regardless if illegal, but even Captain Bligh allowed some fun on his ship of men with grog and ale.

Que tenemos? what do we have?.

Q-Vo!: What's up? Also, as in this instance a happy expression of excitement.

Rainbows: Multi-colored capsules of super potent barbiturates.

Rat: An informer. Someone not to be trusted

Reds: Barbiturates made of seconal, which is very strong, and lethal when mixed with other drugs.

Refer: An older slang term for marijuana.

"Road Dogs": Friends who shared the same experiences and hung out together, taking care of each other.

Rolled up: arrested and detained at a local facility for transfer back to sierra for a disciplinary hearing.

Routered: A rotary woodworking device to level large or small pieces of wood. Much like planing only it can also do corners for decoration and detailed workmanship.

San Ysidro: Border town just North of Tijuana

Santa Nita: A barrio on the West Side of Santa Ana

Scam: A scheme to gain money. To swindle someone out of money.

Scoping: spotting or searching for an area of a safe and easy entrance.

Seconal: Barbiturate, which is very strong and lethal when, mixed with other drugs.

Shook down: A cell search for contraband

Shooting gallery: abandoned house where drugs are used.

SHU unit: secured housing unit for persons at risk

Silver Acres: A barrio in west Santa Ana bordering Garden Grove

Snitch: an informant hated person in the inmate population for telling authorities on criminal activity about to take place

Stinger: a devise for making hot water

Stoned: High on drugs or under the influence of a narcotic.

Swamper: Each crew had a swamper who took care of the equipment, prepared the crew for work detail or fire detail and maintained the base operation or camp.

Tamales: Tasty chili beef & pork covered in a corn meal, and wrapped in cornhusks, served steaming hot.

Tia: aunt

Tio: uncle

Toking: smoking or taking puffs of marijuana

Veterano: veteran or an older experienced person of the jail system.

Vatos: A Mexican rebel, much like a white person would call a surfer a "dude".

Wakeup: just enough dope that is saved for the morning so as not to get sick before you can get some more.

Waterpipe: Device for smoking pot, using water as a coolant.

Wet back: A derogatory term meaning persons illegal entry into the U.S. by way of the Rio Grande.

Printed in the United States
4103